Surgeon Under the Knife

Books by WILLIAM A. NOLEN, M.D.

The Making of a Surgeon
A Surgeon's World
Healing: A Doctor in Search of a Miracle

For younger readers
Spare Parts for the Human Body

Surgeon Under the Knife

William A. Nolen, M.D.

COWARD, McCANN & GEOGHEGAN, INC.
NEW YORK

SBN: 698-10743-8

Library of Congress Cataloging in Publication Data

Nolen, William A.   1928–
   Surgeon under the knife.

   1. Heart Surgery—Personal narratives.   2. Nolen,
William A., 1928–   1. Title. [DNLM: 1. Heart
surgery—Personal narratives. WG168 N791s]
RD598.N512 1976   617'.092'4   75-45470

A portion of Chapter XVI originally appeared in somewhat different form in the March, 1974, issue of *McCall's*. A portion of Chapter III originally appeared in somewhat different form in the February, 1976, issue of *Esquire* under the title "The Attack."

Printed in the United States of America

To Joan

Prologue

When I was a medical student (I graduated from Tufts Medical School in June of 1953), one of the things I was taught was that there was never any urgency about diagnosing brain tumors. If a brain tumor was malignant, then no matter how early you made the diagnosis your chances of curing the patient were almost zero; and if the tumor was benign, no matter how late you made the diagnosis your chances of curing the tumor would still be excellent.

This statement is about as true in 1976 as it was in 1953. Glioblastoma multiforme, the most common of the malignant brain tumors, is still virtually incurable even if you make the diagnosis as soon as the first symptom appears.

Meningiomas, the most common of the benign tumors, are usually surgically curable even if the diagnosis is made late, after symptoms have been present for several months.

In 1953 almost the same sort of thing could have been said about coronary artery disease. At that time there was no such thing as angiography so the diagnosis had to be a tentative and incomplete one, based on the symptom we call angina and on the electrocardiographic findings; but even when the clinical picture and EKG findings were quite specific, treatment was essentially symptomatic. With the proper medications you could temporarily relax the coronary arteries, increase blood flow to the heart, and relieve pain; but there was no treatment that could be used to supply the patient's heart on a permanent or near-permanent basis with the extra blood it needed.

Nor did we, in 1953, know enough about the causes of coronary arteriosclerosis so that we could give the patient advice that might help slow down or even arrest the advancement of the disease. In a sense, as it was with malignant brain tumors so it was with coronary artery disease. There was a bit more urgency about establishing the diagnosis of coronary artery disease, since the physician did have medications and advice to give that could prolong the patient's life, but the urgency wasn't great because the advice and treatment that was available was so limited.

Between 1953 and 1975 that situation has changed markedly. We now have x-ray equipment that permits us to make the diagnosis of coronary artery disease with great accuracy. We have developed techniques that enable us to visualize the coronary arteries and clearly identify any points of obstruction. We still don't know all we'd like to know about the causes of coronary artery disease, but we do know a great deal—enough to slow down and in some cases arrest the process once we've made the diagnosis.

Finally, in 1964, an operation was devised that, though it doesn't remove the block or blocks in the coronary arteries, does enable us to by-pass these points of obstruction and vastly improve, on a permanent or near-permanent basis, the blood supply to the heart muscle. In the years since this óperation, the coronary by-pass, was first performed, advancements in surgical and anesthetic techniques, together with remarkable improvement in the equipment needed to perform the operation, all added to the knowledge that only experience can bring, have brought us to what may be classified as a breakthrough in the treatment of coronary artery disease.

(I am one of those people who is wary of the word "breakthrough." I use it very sparingly. It is a term that refers to a critical point we suddenly reach when after years of labor and innumerable contributions by thousands of men and women working in fields that may have seemed at the time entirely unrelated to what finally ensues, everything comes together to produce one remarkable advance.)

I wish with all my heart (an appropriate phrase) that I had never developed coronary artery disease. But, since I did I am very grateful that I did not develop it till 1975 (i.e. develop the symptoms of the disease; it is impossible to tell how long the arteriosclerotic process in my coronary arteries had been progressing until it reached that critical point where it first produced symptoms). In 1975, when my disease manifested itself, I could go to people who had the knowledge, experience, and equipment to help me. Twenty years ago there would have been no one to whom I could have turned.

9

This book, then, is the story not only of my particular experience as a patient with coronary artery disease but of coronary artery disease in general; of our knowledge of the disease and its treatment as of 1976. It is, I think, a happy, hopeful, optimistic book. I am grateful that I have lived to write it.

Chapter I

Beginning

Most of us would say, if asked, that we want perfect health. We'd be telling the truth as far as the answer goes, but it doesn't go far enough. What we'd have to add, if we were going to be completely honest, is that we'd like to have perfect health, but only under certain conditions. To achieve it we don't want to give up cigarettes, stop drinking alcohol, and drive under fifty miles an hour. We all want perfect health, but only if we can have it without making too many sacrifices. We want it—but only at our price.

Usually, when the gun is at our head our attitude changes. Faced with chronic invalidism or death, we are suddenly willing to do anything that's necessary to remain alive and healthy. But, unfortunately, by then it's often too late. The man with lung cancer isn't going to save his life by giving up cigarettes. The woman whose liver is nothing but a mass of scar tissue isn't going to get over her cirrhosis even if she quits drinking. The boy who broke his neck because the motorcycle he was driving at seventy miles an hour hit a tree isn't going to be able to walk again if he promises to drive slower. For people like these, sadly, it's too late.

As it has been, until 1964, for people like me—a man who lived the first forty-seven years of his life wanting good health, but who wasn't always willing to do everything necessary to have it. As long as I felt well I wasn't overly concerned about what my life-style might be doing to my body, specifically to my coronary arteries. I knew, probably better than most people, since I'm a surgeon, that coronary artery disease develops slowly and insidiously and that often there aren't any warning signs until the arteries are solidly blocked; that, in fact, the first warning sign is often sudden death. But I chose to ignore that knowledge. (Let me say right now, lest this sounds like too much of a *mea culpa* confession, that I have, as you'll see, very few regrets about the way I've lived. But those few are important.)

Fortunately for me and for the hundreds of thousands of people like me, even though I didn't always live as I should have, even though my life-style wasn't sensible as it might have been, even though two arteries to my heart are now almost completely plugged by arteriosclerosis—unlike the patient with advanced lung cancer or liver cirrhosis—I've been given a second chance. How that happened is what this book is all about.

My story begins with a game.

CHAPTER II

May 11, 1975

I have always been an exercise addict. When I say "exercise," I don't mean walking or playing golf; I mean the sort of exertion that makes me perspire and gets my heart racing. When I don't exercise regularly I begin to feel stale and get awfully grouchy. So, at least three times a week and usually more often, I try to get a workout.

In the spring, summer, and fall I play tennis—not well but enthusiastically. In the winter, which in Minnesota sometimes lasts from October until April, I play hockey or racquetball. In the last two years, because it's been increasingly difficult to get a group of adults together to play hockey, I've played more racquetball. After we built a court at the Litchfield Golf Club, in December of 1974, I began playing about five times a week.

Racquetball is a game that requires a lot of physical exertion. It's played indoors in a room forty feet long, twenty feet wide and twenty feet high. The rules are the same as for handball except that the players use short-handled racquets, that look like small tennis rackets. You can hit the ball off any wall or the ceiling but it has to hit the front wall before it hits the floor. Your opponent has to get to the ball and hit it before it hits the floor twice. With all the caroms and bank shots, that ball gets moving awfully fast and a player has to be both quick and fast if he's going to play well. If you were to rate sports in terms of violent exercise on a scale of one to ten, golf would get a one, singles in tennis a six, and racquetball a ten. It's a tough game and I enjoy it.

Until May of 1975 I'd never had any trouble keeping up with my opponents, even the ones twenty or thirty years younger than I am. I couldn't beat them all—I'm not an expert player—but I never lost a match because I couldn't run hard or because I ran out of breath. I could go all-out for an hour, which is about as long as anyone plays singles. Then, after a ten- or fifteen-minute break, I could—and sometimes did—go back onto the court and play doubles for another hour. I think it is reasonable to say that in early May of 1975 I would have been considered, by any standards, to be a forty-seven-year-old man in very good physical condition.

Then, on May 11, 1975, Mother's Day, I had an odd experience. Joan and I had spent the day at our cottage on Lake Minnebelle, six miles outside of Litchfield and at six-thirty that evening we'd gone back to town. I stopped off at the racquetball court to play a match against Dave Gabrielson. Dave is thirty-seven, in good shape, a tough competitor, and I knew I was in for a workout. I'd never played him before—somehow our schedules had never meshed—and I was looking forward to the match.

Dave was already at the racquetball court when I arrived. As we changed into our sweat suits he said, "I'm going to have no mercy on you, Nolen," laughing as he so often does—Dave is a very cheerful guy—and I made some equally unfunny, insipid rejoinder at which we both chuckled. Then we entered the court.

It was an awfully warm day for May in Minnesota; the temperature was in the upper seventies and I had been afraid that the court would be stuffy, but it wasn't. Nor did it seem awfully hot. The twenty-foot ceiling helps to keep the court cool and even without a ventilating fan, which we hadn't yet added, there was room for the air to circulate. We warmed up, hitting the ball off the wall for three or four minutes, and then were ready to play. I won the right to serve first.

When I play racquetball or tennis I always seem to start slow—it takes a while for my shoulder muscles to loosen up—and after about five minutes Dave was ahead six to three.

The score didn't bother me; I knew once I was loose I could easily make up three points, but what was beginning to bother me was that after five minutes I was having a difficult time catching my breath. I just couldn't seem to get my second wind.

Even more unusual, for me, I had a burning sensation down the middle of my chest. I felt as if my windpipe were in spasm and I just couldn't get any air in. I had started to

15

sweat—I perspire easily—but it wasn't the usual hot, soaking sweat; it was what I'd call a cold sweat.

About six minutes into the game I found I couldn't make myself chase down a relatively easy shot that landed behind me in the corner of the court and I had to say, "Dave, I'm sorry, I've got to take a break for a minute. I just can't get going."

"Sure," Dave said, "Nothing serious, is it?"

"No," I said. "I just can't get a second wind. Let's open the outside doors and let some air in here."

We went outside and I sort of crouched in the grass with my head down. After about three minutes the burning sensation in my windpipe went away and I began to feel all right again. "I'm okay now," I said. "Let's get back at it."

"You sure?" Dave asked.

"Sure," I answered. "It must have been the dust in the air. We'll just prop these outside doors open so more air can get in and I'll be all right."

And I was. Once I started playing again the burning didn't come back and I played hard, running all over the court without any trouble. Dave won the first game twenty-one to thirteen but I won the next two twenty-one to eight, twenty-one to twelve. I wanted to quit then—we'd been playing almost an hour—but Dave is a fellow who hates to quit when he's behind and he said "Come on, you son-of-a-gun, we've got time for another game." And, like a damn fool—I'm as much of a competitor as Dave is—I played one more game, a tough one, which he finally won twenty-one to twenty. When we finished, we'd been playing for an hour and a quarter. Dave tried to claim a split but I said, "Bull! I won the match two out of three and you eked out a victory

16

in the consolation. Next time, I won't take it so easy with you.''

We sat around and rested for about ten minutes, then showered and went home.

I was whipped when I came in and just flopped on the couch. "How'd you do?" Joan asked and I told her. I also told her about how I'd run out of gas early in the game.

"You shouldn't be playing racquetball any more now," she said. "It's too hot. Wait till they get a fan in there. Switch to tennis.''

"Maybe you're right," I said. "I guess it was stuffier in there than I realized.''

After lying on the couch for half an hour I felt well rested. I had a beer, then a screwdriver, then a sandwich. I was feeling fine when I went to bed about ten-thirty and I promptly fell asleep.

I didn't realize, of course—or I'd never have fallen off to sleep so easily—that that evening I had had my first attack of angina.

CHAPTER III

Before we get any further into this story, I have to digress for a moment and give the reader the information he or she needs to understand properly what I'm writing about. I want to keep the narrative flowing, so each time I'll only interject as much as is necessary to follow the story to the point I've reached.

I'm going to try to keep this book as free as possible of complicated terms and anatomical descriptions, but there are some medical words, commonly used by the layman but often poorly or incompletely understood, and since they're essential, we may as well get them straight now. Most of this you may know; if so, I apologize for the elaboration.

Angina, which can be properly pronounced an'-gĭ-na or an-gī'-na, is one of these terms. Angina means, simply, heart pain.

The heart is a muscular organ that is divided into four chambers: two atria and two ventricles. The right atrium collects all the unoxygenated blood that flows back from the other organs of the body. From the right atrium this blood flows into the right ventricle, which pumps it out into the small blood vessels that line the air sacs of the lung. While passing though the vessels in the lungs, the blood is resaturated with oxygen.

From the lungs the blood flows back into the left atrium, from which in turn it flows into the left ventricle, the largest chamber and chief pumping mechanism of the heart. When the left ventricle contracts, it drives blood—loaded with oxygen—out into the aorta, the main blood vessel of the body and the one from which all the other arteries of the body (except those to the lungs) originate. Each of the chambers of the heart and the aorta is separated from the other by valves, which, unless diseased, permit blood to flow only in the proper direction.

Every sixty seconds the entire five quarts of blood in the body pass through the heart. Put another way, in every twenty-four-hour period the heart pumps 2,600 gallons of blood.

Unfortunately, and incongruous as it seems with all this blood passing through the heart, not much reaches the heart muscle itself.

The heart muscle receives its blood from two arteries, the coronary arteries, which originate just outside the heart proper in the first half-inch of the aorta. When the left ventricle contracts and drives blood out into the aorta and on to the rest of the body, the aortic valve cusps (of which there are normally three) are pushed against the aortic wall. These cusps block their openings so that no (or very little) blood flows into the coronary arteries when the heart is contracting. When the heart relaxes between beats, the aortic valves fall away from the wall of the aorta, preventing blood from regurgitating into the ventricle, and blood then can and does flow into the openings of the coronary arteries, providing the oxygenated blood that the heart muscle needs to do its work. The coronary arteries are the only arteries in the body that fill when the heart relaxes and empty when the heart contracts.

The two coronary arteries are known as the left and right coronaries. The right coronary supplies mainly the right and back sides of the ventricles. The left coronary supplies the left side, the front, and part of the back of the heart muscle. Each of these arteries gives off branches that may or may not overlap the blood supply of the other artery.

Each coronary artery measures two to three millimeters (2/25" to 3/25") at its origin, a little smaller in circumference than the ordinary drinking straw. As the arteries extend out into the heart, they become progressively more narrow.

The right coronary artery usually gives off one fairly large branch, but most of its branches are relatively small. The left main coronary artery divides, about an inch from its origin, into two main divisions. These are the circumflex artery, which runs from the front around the left side to the back of the heart, and the left anterior descending artery, which runs down the front of the heart and supplies much of the blood to that very important left ventricle. (For those who would like to see a picture of all this, turn to the illustration on page 126).

Now, back to angina. Heart pain, to which we will refer from now on as angina, develops when the heart muscle is not receiving enough oxygen to do the work it has to do. Sometimes, although rarely, the heart muscle won't get enough oxygen because the oxygen saturation of the blood is too low. For example, a patient with a perfectly normal heart and wide-open coronary arteries might develop angina if he was immersed in an atmosphere in which the air contained less than the normal 21 percent oxygen (air is usually 78 percent nitrogen). A normal individual who was suddenly transported to the top of the Himalayas and immediately made to run a mile might also develop angina because his blood hasn't had time to thicken (to use a common term); that is, develop more hemoglobin per unit so that each drop of blood will contain more oxygen, a necessary adjustment at high altitudes where the oxygen concentration in the air is lower than at sea level or at the normal elevations where most of us live.

But these are rare causes for angina and I mention them only for the sake of completeness. Most often angina occurs because not enough blood can get to the heart muscle when the heart muscle needs it. And the reason the blood can't get to the heart muscle is because one or more of the coronary arteries has become partly or completely blocked by arteriosclerosis and there just isn't room for the blood to get through the artery.

Angina is really a warning sign. It's the heart's way of saying, "Hold it! You're asking me to do more work for you than I can do with the blood supply you're giving me.

Either slow down, or figure out some way to get more blood to me."

Typical angina pain is usually located beneath the sternum (the breastbone) and the patient often describes it as "squeezing" or "as if someone was sitting on my chest." Sometimes the pain radiates into the jaw or the teeth. Often it goes into the left shoulder and down the left arm, usually to the side of the little finger. More rarely (in about 10 percent of cases) it will go into the right shoulder or arm.

Usually, when a patient first develops angina, the pain will come on when he's exerting himself and will go away when he rests. Maybe the first time he'll notice it is when he walks a mile at a fast pace. Perhaps for weeks, months, or even years, it won't get any worse or come on any more easily. But, usually, once it starts it will progress, sometimes very slowly, sometimes quite rapidly; it depends on whether any further narrowing develops in the patient's coronary arteries.

If he first notices angina—which he probably won't recognize as such immediately—after jogging a mile, a month later he may notice it after a half-mile. Then he may notice it if he walks fast for a couple of blocks. Finally, he'll decide something is wrong and go to his doctor. His doctor, possibly on the basis of the history, perhaps with the aid of some special tests we'll get to later, will tell him he has angina and discuss the treatment (which, again, we'll get to later in great detail).

It's important to point out here that an attack of angina, though it may be and often is referred to as a heart attack, is not truly a heart attack in the sense that physicians use the phrase.

Pains in the chest are extremely common, and a few

words are necessary here about chest pains in general. Most are innocuous, the result of minor strains of the muscles and nerves that lie between the ribs. The difficulty lies in distinguishing these harmless chest pains, which can safely be ignored, from those chest pains that may be caused by heart trouble.

"Typical" angina pain can be diagnosed with ease and accuracy by any first-year medical student, but when the angina is not typical it can be misdiagnosed by the most astute and experienced cardiologists. Pain that is seemingly unrelated to the heart—but is in fact anginal in origin—is sometimes called an anginal equivalent.

The patient who has had an attack of angina has not killed any of his heart muscle. The heart pain began when the blood supply got too low for the demand on the heart muscle; with rest the demand for blood decreased and the pain went away. If you took an electrocardiogram, an electrical tracing of the heart, before the attack of angina and after, they would look the same. There would be no evidence that any muscle had been damaged.

What physicians usually refer to as a heart attack is what is technically known as an infarct. When an infarct occurs, a segment of the heart muscle becomes completely and irreversibly (with exceptions we'll note later) deprived of its blood supply. At first, while the muscle is dying, the pain is like that of angina. But it doesn't relent with rest. Once the muscle has died and, hopefully, begun to convert to scar tissue, the pain goes away.

For example, it is not unusual for angina or an infarct to cause shoulder pain. Not infrequently the physician diagnoses this pain as bursitis and proceeds to treat it with aspirin, heat, and possibly cortisone injections into the shoulder. Six months or a year later an EKG taken for a new pain or as part of a routine physical reveals evidence of an old infarct, probably an infarct that had been the real cause of the shoulder pain. A patient whose angina radiates into his arm is often told initially that he is suffering from neuritis, for which he may be given vitamin shots. And hundreds of patients have had perfectly normal teeth removed from their lower jaw in an attempt to relieve pain that was misinterpreted as toothache but that was, in fact, angina. Both patient and doctor must be very wary or at one time or another they are going to miss the diagnosis of angina, with potentially fatal consequences.

My father, at the age of fifty-five, had suffered for two years from recurrent episodes of severe pain in his lower jaw. He was seen by some of the brightest internists and most astute neurologists in Massachusetts. None of them could find a satisfactory explanation for his pain. Finally, in desperation, he had all the lower teeth in the left side of his jaw removed. The pain was not relieved.

In retrospect, knowing that he continued to have episodes of jaw pain till he died at fifty-eight of heart disease, I am as certain as I can be that his pain problem, through the last five years of his life, was almost certainly due to angina.

Although, overall, 85 percent of coronary artery disease occurs in men, women in the postmenopausal years are almost as likely to develop the disease as are males in the same age group; it is the female hormone, estrogen, that in some manner that is not yet clear protects women from arteriosclerosis.

When women do develop coronary artery disease they will, unlike men, almost invariably have one or more angina attacks before they are stricken by an infarct. Again, the explanation for this is not clear. It may be related to the later onset of coronary arteriosclerosis in women, which allows time, in their premenopausal years, for collateral blood vessels to develop.

Almost—a word doctors use incessantly, and with good reason—invariably, angina is brought on by exertion and goes away when the patient rests. But exertion does not always mean that the patient is walking, running, or shoveling snow. Eating is a form of exertion as is sexual intercourse. Any activity that requires a shifting of blood from one area of the body to another (eating draws blood to the digestive tract, intercourse draws it to the pelvic organs) may cause angina. If the chest pain that you experience falls into this "typical" pattern, then consultation with a physician is in order.

For the other, much more common, chest pains, there are a few things you can do to reassure yourself that the pains are not serious. First, you can see if they are aggravated by motion: by twisting or turning or in some other way stretching the sore area. If this aggravates the pain, it's probably simply an irritable nerve or stretched muscle.

Similarly, if the pain feels very superficial or if it's relieved by a heating pad, it's almost certainly innocuous.

If it's a sharp pain caused by taking a deep breath, and if it diminishes in intensity when you exhale it's almost certainly unrelated to your heart. Quick, sharp chest pains are very common and usually innocuous.

If it's a pain just like pains you've had before, which went away spontaneously or after taking a couple of aspirin, it's certainly safe to ignore it.

I am trying here to be as helpful as I can be, to reassure

patients so that they don't go running to the doctor with every sore rib or chest muscle. I don't like using phrases like "almost certainly" or "highly likely," but I hope you understand that I have to. Medicine is always an uncertain business and only the inexperienced or ignorant physician writes or speaks dogmatically.

Finally, let me say this: I have had hundreds of episodes of chest pain in my life, as have all the men and women I have ever known. I worried transiently about some of them, but invariably they went away or diminished so that I never sought medical attention for them. When I finally developed angina, even though I didn't recognize it as such immediately, I did know that this was not the usual, harmless, "garden variety" chest pain. I sensed at once that this pain was something new, something that might eventually require medical consultation.

I suspect that most people, when they develop true angina, recognize it as a "different" sort of pain with more serious implications than their usual innocuous chest pains.

An infarct may occur when a narrow area in a blood vessel, one that may have previously caused angina, becomes completely occluded so that not enough blood can get through the artery to provide adequate oxygen for the heart. Sometimes this happens because a clot develops in the channel that has already been narrowed by arteriosclerosis. Unfortunately, infarcts often occur in patients who have never had any warning that there was anything the matter with their coronary arteries. For some reason—perhaps because the patient has rarely if ever exerted himself physically—he never had any previous angina.

Angina rarely kills a patient; the only exceptions are those rare ones in which the area partly deprived of blood is one through which the nervous system of the heart runs, so that the angina triggers an incapacitating, fatal malfunction of the beat of the heart.

An infarct, on the other hand, may and often does kill the victim quite promptly, often within a matter of seconds or minutes. Whether the infarct is fatal will depend on the size of the vessel involved—i.e., how large and important a segment of the heart muscle it supplies—and on the collateral circulation. By collateral circulation I mean those branches arising from unoccluded vessels that may supply some—possibly quite a lot—of blood to the same area that the newly occluded vessel once reached.

The person who suffers a sudden complete occlusion of his left main or left anterior descending coronary artery will probably not live more than a few minutes. The man who suffers an occlusion of a small branch of the circumflex artery will suffer the death of some of his heart muscle, but he himself will probably survive. How well the heart functions after an infarct will depend on how much muscle the infarct has destroyed.

In a way—and you couldn't have convinced me of this before Mother's Day, 1975—angina is sort of a blessing; it warns you that something is wrong with the circulation to your heart. If you heed the warning, you have a chance to hold onto both your life and your health.

Chapter IV

May 12, 1975–June 17, 1975

The morning after my Mother's Day game with Dave I woke feeling fine and was at the hospital by 7:45. Since it's relevant to this whole story, perhaps this is as good a time as any to tell you how I earn my living.

I'm a general surgeon in the city of Litchfield (population, 5,232), Meeker County (population, 20,000, give or take a couple of thousand), Minnesota. I've been in practice here ever since I finished my surgical training at Bellevue Hospital in 1960.

I'm the chief of surgery at our Meeker County Hospital and have been ever since I arrived in the city. (Some cynics have suggested that this is because I am the only surgeon in

Meeker County.) The active staff of our hospital is comprised of eleven other doctors, of whom ten are G.P.s and one an internist. All the G.P.s do some surgery, usually relatively minor cases such as hernia repairs, hemorrhoids, and vein strippings. Some of the G.P.s also do bigger surgery—cholecystectomies (gallbladder removals) and hysterectomies, for example. But for all the major surgery—cancers of the bowel or stomach, insertion of artificial hip prostheses, chest cases—I'm usually asked to operate. Six of the G.P.s and I are associated in a partnership called the Litchfield Clinic, but I get on well with all the other doctors on the staff so all of them, when the case is an appropriate one, ask me to help.

As you'd expect, this gives me a reasonably full operative work load, about five hundred cases a year as compared to the hundred and fifty or so cases the average general surgeon does. (One more note: Because of the proliferation of subspecialists in surgery, the "general" surgeon in a big city is often in fact an abdominal surgeon. Since there are no orthopedists, gynecologists, urologists, or any other surgical subspecialists in Meeker County, I remain a "general" surgeon in the old and true sense of the word.)

On a typical day—and this Monday was fairly typical—I get up about seven thirty, wash, dress, and get to the hospital about five minutes of eight, just in time to say hello to the first patient I'm going to operate on that morning, who, by the time I arrive, is on the operating-room table waiting to be put to sleep.

From eight until ten thirty or eleven or later, depending on how many patients I have on the operative schedule, I operate. Between operations I visit the patients I have in the hospital to check on the various stages of their postoperative progress. I don't generally eat any breakfast but I do drink instant decaffeinated coffee in the doctor's dressing room when I get a chance. If I have a long wait between cases—because, for example, some other doctor is doing a tonsillectomy or a hernia, I may work on an article or book that I'm writing. I always bring a pad and pencil with me to the doctor's dressing room. The secret to combining careers as both surgeon and writer seems to me to depend to a great extent on wasting as little time as possible, particularly in the morning. I'm a morning person and those morning hours are precious to me.

If I'm through operating by ten thirty or eleven, I go back to our clinic, which is two doors from my home and, unless there's some emergency like a cut hand or a minor fracture that I have to take care of, I spend the hour or hour and a half until noon writing.

At noon I usually play racquetball or tennis, depending on the season. I'm home by one thirty, when I may have a light snack, lie down and read the paper, and go back to the clinic by two or two fifteen. I see patients from then till five, but since a surgeon's office practice is apt to be relatively light, I try to see most of my patients on Wednesday or Friday afternoons. On the other afternoons I see occasional drop-ins that my partners are too busy to see (I'm not the sort of specialist who is too proud to do camp physicals), take care of minor injuries, farm or industrial accidents that are a regular but unscheduleable part of every day, and try to read or skim all the medical and surgical journals that a doctor has to at least peruse if he isn't going to fall hopelessly behind.

At five I leave the clinic and go back to the hospital and

31

check briefly on the patients I operated on in the morning, particularly if they've had major surgery.

Then I may go and watch one of my children participate in some school event, a track meet or a football game perhaps. After that I go home and, unless there's something special scheduled, Joan and I have a drink or two, eat, and spend the evening reading. I usually get to bed about ten thirty.

Sometimes, when I can manage to keep my operating schedule clear for a morning (usually by doubling up on cases on other days), I take a morning off just to write, when I have an article due or am working on a book perhaps.

And, of course, there are times when I have to get away from Litchfield, either because I need a vacation or have speaking or book-promotion obligations. On those occasions one of the four surgeons who practice in Willmar (thirty-five miles west of Litchfield) covers for me. Sometimes my associates send the patient to Willmar; sometimes the surgeon will come to Litchfield and operate. I've always tried to keep extended trips to a minimum, but when book writing (with the consequent necessary promotional trips) became a bigger part of my life, I found that about once a year I'd have to be away two, three, or even four weeks at a time. I didn't like this, but I accepted it as necessary.

My wife Joan and I have six children—Jim, twenty-one (working); Jody, twenty (a junior at Yale); Billy, nineteen (a sophomore at Harvard); Annie, seventeen (a senior at Litchfield High); Julius, sixteen (a junior at Litchfield High); and Mary, thirteen (an eighth grader)—so you will understand when I say that our days and evenings are endless in their variety, though less so since the kids have gotten older and begun to leave home. It's rare, for example, that even the three children who live with us are around for dinner at the same time.

And, surgery being the unpredictable profession that it is, typical days aren't really typical. I may spend my lunch break working on a patient with a broken arm or ruptured spleen; instead of going to bed at ten thirty, I may go to the hospital to repair a strangulated hernia. If I do have to operate through the noon hours, then I may switch the tennis to five thirty. I make whatever adjustments I can.

I realized, back on that May 11, Mother's Day, that my life was full, but felt that I had it in as much control as I could reasonably expect. Basically, but with some key reservations (important ones) that we'll get to later, I still think that was the case.

On this particular Monday I had a tennis match lined up for noon, but a farmer caught his hand in some farm machinery at 11 A.M. and I spent my lunch hour repairing tendons and fractured bones. Tuesday it rained, so I missed my workout again and it wasn't till noon on Wednesday that I got to the tennis court. Almost every Wednesday noon Stan Roeser, one of my closest friends, and I play tennis. He is a co-owner of the local weekly newspaper and he writes most of the news and features. The paper is "put to bed" (as they say in the newspaper world) on Tuesday evening, so Wednesday is his day to relax. Stan and I have certainly played each other several hundred times over the last ten years, and though it ought to be obvious to any knowledgeable tennis buff that I am the superior player (it's certainly obvious to me), Stan somehow manages to win almost half our matches; he claims 60 percent, but I deny that and he has no proof. We always have very close matches.

33

By the time I started playing on Wednesday I'd all but forgotten about my experience on the racquetball court on Sunday. I'd had no more shortness of breath, no more chest pain, and was certain that my brief episode of trouble had been due to the stale air in the court.

So it came as a real surprise—almost a shock—to me when, as we were finishing our third game, about ten minutes into the match, I noticed the burning sensation in my throat again. I didn't say anything and I took my time as we changed ends of the court in the hope that it would go away. But it didn't; in fact, it got worse. In the fourth game Stan hit a drop shot that I should have gotten to easily, but I just couldn't push myself to it. "Stan," I said, "I'm sorry, but I've got to take a break. I just can't run, can't seem to get my second wind. I've got a burning sensation in my throat. Same thing happened to me Sunday, playing Gabrielson in racquetball. Just give me a couple of minutes to catch my breath and I'm sure I'll be all right again."

"You sure you want to go on?" he said. "It's just a game, you know."

"Baloney, it's just a game," I said. "We're going on all right, and I'm going to beat you. Just give me a minute."

After what was certainly no more than three minutes, I was able to play again. I got my second wind, and even though I lost the first set to Stan six to four, I came back and won the second seven to six. By then it was one thirty and I had to go home so I'd have time to shower and change before I went to the office; if I hadn't had to leave, I really felt as if I could have played and won the deciding set.

"Well, that's the last time you pull that on me," Stan said. "All this bullshit about chest pain. I know you, you just pulled that so I'd let up on you. I'm tempted to mark this one down as a victory."

"Go ahead," I said. "It will certainly be your last win over me this season." Tennis players—jocks in general, I guess—are given to this sort of humorous (I use the word loosely), good-natured bantering. It's all part of the game.

I went home, showered, read the paper and—though I didn't really feel tired—did lie down for a short nap, getting to the clinic at two thirty. I saw patients all afternoon and had no trouble. I really wasn't concerned. The possibility that I might have heart disease still seemed to me very unlikely.

This lack of concern wasn't due to ignorance, at least not entirely. As a surgeon, I didn't treat patients with angina or infarcts but, like every doctor, I know a reasonable amount about heart disease. It's so terribly widespread that no matter what specialty you practice, some of your patients are certain to have heart disease along with the problem for which you're treating them. Certainly many of the patients on whom I operate have or have had heart ailments of one kind or another, and I have to know enough about the sick heart to manage it intelligently while I'm giving them surgical care.

I can't say that the possibility my distress might be due to heart disease hadn't entered my head; it had, of course. I don't believe there's an adult male in the entire country who hasn't wondered, at one time or another, whether some pain or other symptom in his chest wasn't due to heart trouble. After all, not a day goes by that there aren't reports of sudden death due to "heart attacks" in the obituary columns of the newspapers or the news magazine. I knew it was a common ailment, and I knew, for reasons we'll get to soon, that I was a good candidate for the disease. But I did not think, at this time, my symptoms were coming from my heart.

There were two reasons why I discounted the possibility. First, the distress I was having was not like any angina I'd heard of or read about. There was no squeezing pain, just a burning sensation. And it didn't radiate down my left arm or into my jaw, as the pain of angina often does. If I were having angina, it was a very atypical kind.

Second, if I were having attacks of angina I didn't think I could possibly have resumed playing tennis or racquetball after a three-minute rest and then have continued to play hard for another hour without any more distress. Angina, as I knew it, went away with rest but came right back with a resumption of exercise. When my pain stayed away after a brief rest, I concluded it wasn't angina.

It happens that I was wrong in my conclusions; I didn't know as much about angina as I thought I did, but I learned more later.

I continued to play tennis on pleasant days, and racquetball on rainy ones. I was still beating the opponents I usually beat and losing to the players that regularly beat me. Only now, invariably, about five minutes into any match I'd have to take a break and get what I had come to call my second wind.

Finally one evening, after a very tough racquetball match against Keith Langmo, one of my regular opponents, as we were resting before taking our showers, Keith said, "Damn it, Bill, you may say you feel all right now, but you sure as hell don't look it. You're white as a sheet."

And Stan Roeser, who had been watching us play, said, "Listen, Bill, if you had a patient who was having the trouble you're having, you'd sure as hell send him to an internist, wouldn't you?"

"I suppose so," I said. "But, damn it, I know it can't be my heart. If it were, how could I come back after a five-minute rest and play hard for another hour? If I were having angina I'd have dropped dead on the court weeks ago."

"Well, maybe it isn't your heart," Keith said, "but surer than hell something's screwed up. Why don't you use your head and go see somebody? It's getting so everyone out here is afraid to play you for fear you'll kill yourself."

"Bull," I said. "I didn't notice you letting up in that second game."

"Of course not," Keith laughed. "I'm not so worried that I'm going to let you beat me. But, seriously, why don't you go see someone?"

"Okay," I said, "I guess you're right. Even if it isn't my heart I have to admit it must be something and I'd better get over it. I'll call someone tomorrow."

The next day, Tuesday, June 17, I called Bill Petersen, an internist who practices in Minneapolis.

Bill is the kind of doctor you can't help liking. Even though he has a very busy practice, he never makes you feel as if he were in a hurry. When he comes into the examining room to see you he sits down, stretches out, and acts as if he had the entire afternoon to spend with you. It's an attitude you don't find in many doctors. Like me, most doctors always seem to be in a hurry, anxious to get away from the patient. We should be more like Bill.

Bill and I know each other well. Over the fifteen years I've lived in Minnesota, Bill has treated me on those few occasions when I've had medical problems that my partners preferred not to treat. I not only like Bill, I have great respect for his clinical judgment.

The only relatively serious medical problem I've ever had has been high blood pressure. I have what is called labile hypertension, which means that my blood pressure goes up very easily in response to any physical or emotional stress, but it also cames down when I relax. Until about ten years ago doctors didn't worry much about patients with labile hypertension. We assumed that such patients probably had relatively normal blood pressures most of the time and that occasional spurts of hypertension probably didn't do any significant harm. Now we know that this isn't so. Studies have shown that patients with labile hypertension who are not treated are more likely to develop the complications of high blood pressure—principally heart attacks and strokes—than are those labile hypertensives who are treated.

In my case it seemed particularly wise to treat my labile hypertension, since my father had been a labile hypertensive all his life and had died of an apparent infarct at the age of fifty-eight. Coronary artery disease tends to run in families. Bill had supervised the management of my blood pressure problems over the last fifteen years. (I may as well admit now that my blood pressure problems weren't as well managed as they should have been. The fault was mine, not Bill's. I absolutely dreaded having a blood pressure cuff wrapped on my arm. I was convinced, and probably rightly so, that simply wrapping the cuff on was enough to raise my blood pressure thirty points. So I'd go for a year at a time without having anyone check to make certain my blood pressure wasn't getting out of control. I behaved, to put it succinctly, like a typical high-blood-pressure patient.)

Nevertheless, despite my neglect of my blood pressure, I was in good physical condition.

I had been to Bill for a complete physical in November, 1974. I'm not one of those people who believe in an annual physical; my philosophy, generally, has been, "If you feel well, don't go looking for trouble." I know this isn't the advice most doctors give their patients—I guess it's not really the advice I give my patients either but I know it's the policy most doctors, at least the ones I know, follow for themselves. If there's a doctor who practices in Litchfield who undergoes an annual physical, I don't know who he is. I do know that last year I asked Lennox Danielson, a robust, active G.P. of seventy-one, when he'd had his last physical and he said, "Gee, I don't know. About forty years ago, I guess, when I had palpitations off and on for a few weeks."

The reason I'd gone to Bill in November of 1974, for the first time in about ten years, was because I knew I was going to have to go on a book-promoting trip shortly after the first of the year and I also knew my blood pressure was up a bit. I wanted to get it under control before I went on the road; those book-promotion trips are very strenuous excursions.

Anyway, my physical examination that November had been very reassuring. I had, more or less, "the works"— complete history and physical examination, routine lab work, electrocardiogram. I even had a Master's two-step, a test during which you run up and down a couple of stairs while the EKG (electrocardiograph) wires are attached to

39

you, to see if your heart shows any evidence of change during exercise.

"Your blood pressure's running a little high," Bill said, "about 150/94 (normal limits are up to 140/90) so I think I'll change your medication around a little. Otherwise you're in very good shape."

"What about my weight?" I asked. "I know I've gained a few pounds."

"Yeah, you're up to 196. You were 185 ten years ago. It wouldn't do you any harm to cut back a little, but you're so much less fat than some of the patients I see that it's hard for me to get excited."

I thanked Bill and left. When he sent me a follow-up letter a week later, with my lab reports, he noted, "You'll see your cholesterol is actually below normal, which is of course excellent. Unfortunately, the lab forgot to check your triglycerides (another sort of coronary artery disease-related fatty substance found in the blood), so the next time you're in town stop in and we'll get one done; or, if you prefer, go to your own lab and have it done."

Naturally, so delighted was I with the negative physical examination, the normal electrocardiogram, and the low blood cholesterol, that I never did bother to get my triglycerides checked. And, of course, this nice, reassuring negative physical had been done in November, five months before I'd begun having my strange "burning."

CHAPTER V

June 17, 1975–June 18, 1975

On June 17, a Tuesday, I called Bill Petersen and told him about the strange episodes I'd been experiencing on the tennis court. When I finished I said, "I'm sure it can't be angina, but since I don't know what it is and all these people seem to be getting worried about me, I thought I'd better call."

"I'm glad you did," Bill said. "You may be right. It could be something simple but we've got to look into it. If ever in the world there's a type A personality (driving, inclined to be tense, prone to heart disease) you're it. When can you come down to see me?"

"Well," I said, "I promised to do an interview on paranormal healing for the educational station at the University of Minnesota, and that's on the schedule for nine tomorrow morning. After ten I'm free. But I realize you're probably booked solid, so let me know when you want me to come. I'll be around all month and I'll make it at your convenience."

"No, you don't," Bill said. "You're not weaseling out that easily. It so happens I have to do a stress EKG at Jonson Hospital tomorrow at eight thirty. You ought to be able to get from the university to Jonson easily by ten fifteen. I'll book you for ten thirty. I'll call Jonson right away to make certain I can set it up. If I don't call you back in ten minutes, I'll see you at Jonson in the morning."

"Fine," I said, "if it doesn't inconvenience you."

"Don't worry about me," Bill said. "You just get your butt down here tomorrow. False alarm or not, we aren't taking any chances."

Bill didn't call back, so that evening Joan and I drove the sixty-five miles into Minneapolis. We had decided to spend the night in a hotel to avoid getting up early for the drive down in the morning. I didn't want to be tired when I took the stress test.

In all honesty, I have to say that I was relaxed as we drove into Minneapolis. I felt so well, and my symptoms were so atypical of any angina pain I'd ever heard of, that I just couldn't believe I had a heart problem. I thought perhaps Bill might find I had some strange kind of asthma for which I could take a bronchodilator (a pill or spray to loosen up the windpipe) before I did any vigorous exercise. We stopped and had a cheerful dinner at a restaurant on the outskirts of Minneapolis and we were in bed at the hotel by ten thirty in the evening.

42

The next morning I got up about eight, drove
University of Minnesota television station,
twenty-minute interview on faith healing, and
terview was over, drove up and checked in
Hospital outpatient department. I was nice
least as relaxed as I ever am.

Now I have to explain how a stress electrocardiogram is
done. First, the technician shaves appropriate spots on the
patient's chest and abdomen and sticks electrocardiographic lead wires to these spots with an adhesive. Then, with the
patient resting, a baseline EKG is recorded.

Next, the patient stands up and the technician starts a
treadmill going. The speed of the treadmill and the pitch of
the treadmill can be altered by the technician. The treadmill
is always started at a very slow rate and a minimal incline,
so that the patient can easily adjust to walking on it as it
turns. At regular intervals the speed and/or the pitch of the
incline of the treadmill is increased so that it takes progressively more exertion on the part of the patient to keep walking on the treadmill. And all the time that this is being done,
the electrocardiographic tracing shows what is happening
to the heart rate, which, with exertion, will naturally be increasing. The electrocardiogram will also show any evidence of heart irregularities or changes in the pattern of the
heart waves that might be evidence that all is not well with
the heart; i.e., that under conditions of stress the heart cannot function as it should. These are usually signs that the
heart is not getting sufficient oxygen to meet its demands
under conditions of stress, and are fairly definite evidence
that either one or more of the arteries to the heart is partially or completely blocked; or, more unlikely, that the heart
valves are not functioning as they should. The pattern of

the changes, when examined by a physician well versed in electrocardiography, will give him a fairly good idea what, if anything, is wrong with the heart.

It's possible that the stress induced by the exercise on the treadmill will cause not only angina but an infarct, so stress EKGs are done with caution. Technicians run the machines, but a physician who can interpret EKGs is always in attendance to treat any patient who develops an acute problem, or to halt the test if it becomes obvious that it is dangerous to continue.

My resting pulse—my heart rate when I'm just sitting around reading or relaxing—is generally between sixty-four and seventy-two. I've always considered this fairly good evidence that I have a relatively healthy heart, one with efficient muscles. Athletes, long-distance runners in particular, may get their resting pulses down into the high forties or low fifties. In other words, at rest, beating only fifty times a minutes, their hearts are able to pump enough blood to their bodies to keep them functioning and healthy. Anyone with a basically healthy heart, by regular exercise, should be able to increase the heart's efficiency and get it down into the seventy-to-eighty-beats-a-minute range. On the other hand, the patient who rarely if ever exercises may find that his or her resting pulse is in the nineties.

It's also true that it takes more exertion to increase substantially the heart rate of someone who exercises regularly than it does to increase the heart rate of a sedentary person. An athlete with a resting pulse of 60/minute may raise his pulse to 70/minute after walking up two flights of stairs rather quickly. The nonexerciser, with a resting pulse of 90/minute, may find his pulse at 130/minute after going up two flights of stairs at the same rate.

Anyway, my resting pulse and my pulse at exercise, which I check every now and then, have always led me to believe I had a healthy, efficient heart.

The technician explained the stress test to me, Bill Petersen came in and we said hello; and when I stepped on the slow-moving treadmill, my initial pulse rate was 75. Depending on the age, height, and weight of the patient, a goal is generally set before the stress test is begun; i.e., the technician will plan to increase the stress of the test at regular intervals until the patient's pulse reaches a certain predetermined level. If at that time the patient has no symptoms and the electrocardiogram shows no changes, then the stress test is considered negative; i.e., there is no evidence of any heart disease. In my particular case the preset figure was 186 beats a minute. If I got my pulse to 186 with no symptoms or changes in my EKG (except rate, of course), it would be assumed my heart was normal and healthy.

I didn't make it. I started on the treadmill with a pulse of 75/minute and a normal EKG. Once I was used to the treadmill, after two minutes, the pace and incline were increased. My pulse went to 110, but I felt fine and the EKG stayed normal. After a second increase in speed and pitch, I began to perspire and I said to Bill, panting, "I'm beginning to feel that burning sensation I get on the tennis court. Not bad, but it's there." Bill said nothing.

Another increase in stress and a few seconds later I said, "The burning's getting worse. It's when it gets like this that I usually have to take a break for a few minutes." I was sweating and again it was a cold sweat, not the kind of healthy, warm perspiration I'd learned to expect when exercising.

"Okay," Bill said, "hold it." The technician turned off

45

the treadmill and I stepped off and flopped on the bed near the machine.

"How's the pain?" Bill asked.

"Still there," I said. "In fact, it's a little bit worse." I was still hooked up to the EKG.

Another half-minute or so and Bill, who was watching both me and the EKG tracing, said, "How's it now?"

"Better," I answered. "Not gone, but better." I was still flopped out on the couch.

A couple of minutes later I sat up. "All gone now," I said. "In fact, I could probably get back on that damn machine."

"No way," said Bill. "You sit there a few minutes and rest up." He threw me a towel. "Dry yourself off. You'll feel better. Your pulse is back almost to normal now."

I sat on the bed for another five minutes, getting my wind back, feeling better all the time. Bill, in the meantime, was reviewing the EKG's that had been run during my test. Finally the technician came over and took the EKG wires off me. I went into the bathroom, washed my face, and then came back and sat on the edge of the bed. Bill brought the EKGs over, sat beside me, and started to go over them. "I know you're one of those cutting-type doctors," he said, "but even a surgeon ought to be able to see what we've got here."

"Changes?" I said.

Bill nodded. "Changes, no question and fairly prominent."

"Trouble?" I asked.

"Who knows?" Bill said. "But I'd be less than honest if I didn't say, probably. In fact, almost certainly. Maybe one in ten times we get a stress EKG that's a false positive. We do more studies and find it's all a mistake. But not with the kind of changes you've got."

I won't bore you with the details, partly because I'm no EKG expert and I didn't really understand everything Bill showed me, but the evidence was clear. My EKG was normal until my heart rate (same as pulse rate) reached 122 beats a minute. It was when I got to 122 that my burning sensation had begun, and it was at 122 that changes in the normal mountain valley-type tracings of the EKG had begun to appear. By the time my rate reached 156, the point at which I had said, "It's about here that I'd ask for a break if this were a tennis game," and the stress test had been terminated, the changes were much more marked. For the first minute or two of my rest period, when the burning had continued to increase, the changes persisted and became even a bit more apparent. Then, as my pain or burning (I still don't know how to describe it) gradually decreased and disappeared, the abnormal EKG patterns disappeared, too. When my pulse was back to 85, when my pain was all gone, my EKG looked like that of a perfectly normal individual.

"What do you think, Bill?" I said.

"No question," he answered. "You need an angiogram. We've got to see what those blood vessels look like. You know George Smith, don't you?" (George Smith is not his real name.)

"Yes," I said. "I met him a few weeks ago when I came down here to watch Frank Johnson do a coronary by-pass. I even watched one of his partners do an angiogram."

"Did you like him?" Bill asked.

"Sure," I said, "he seemed like a nice guy."

"Shall I arrange to have him do your angiogram?"

"Might as well," I said.

"Let me give him a call right now," he said. "I think he's at Brooks Hospital."

While Bill waited for George Smith to answer the page,

he said to me, "Knowing you, you'll probably want to get this done as quickly as possible. If George can put you in tonight and do the angio tomorrow, do you want to go ahead?"

I thought for a few seconds, then said, "I just don't know, Bill. This whole thing is sort of a shock. Billy had just gotten back from Harvard when I had to go east to speak at a medical-school graduation. Now he's up at Telemark (a resort lodge in northwest Wisconsin, where Joan and I and the kids go whenever I can get away) teaching tennis and we sort of planned to spend the weekend up there. Do you think it would be safe to wait?"

"Sure," Bill said. "You're really not having any symptoms unless you push an awful lot. I just wanted to let you get it out of the way if you wanted to."

Just then George answered the page. Bill explained about my test and then put me on to talk to him.

"Looks like I caught something from you guys when I was down here a couple of weeks ago," I said.

"Sounds like it," George said. "But remember—about 10 percent of the time, even with a positive stress test, the angio turns out negative."

"I know that," I said, "and I'll be praying I'm in that 10 percent category. When can you do me?"

"When will you be back from Telemark?"

"Tomorrow's Thursday and we're leaving Litchfield after I finish operating. We'll probably come back Monday night. What if I came down on Tuesday, June 24? Could you do me on Wednesday, June 25?"

"No problem," George said. "Get in about noon. Come to Brooks. I'll put you in under my name."

"Fine," I said. "Thanks."

"No trouble at all," he said. "Sorry it has to be done."

I went into the washroom of the examining room where the stress EKG had been done and started to put on my clothes.

"How you feeling now?" Bill asked.

I had difficulty answering. I was choked up, on the verge of tears. Finally I sort of croaked, "Physically, okay. Mentally, I've got to admit it's a blow. I'm depressed. I really didn't think I'd have anything the matter with me."

"I know," Bill said. "It's a damn shame. But there's nothing to do but go ahead and see it through."

"I agree," I said. "I'll be hoping it's a false alarm but I don't think it is and I know you don't either. But, whatever it is, I've got to face it."

"Yes," Bill said, "and if you've done the reading, you know there's a lot that can be done now that couldn't have been done ten years ago."

"Right," I said. I was dressed now and had myself under emotional control. I thanked the technician who had run the test and then Bill walked with me to the parking lot.

"I'll be in touch," he said. "George will have you on his service, but I'll be in to see you Tuesday. Don't overdo up at Telemark. I'd definitely stay away from singles. Try doubles if you want, but if you have any symptoms, quit."

"I'll be careful," I said. "Don't worry. I want to be around for a while yet." We shook hands, said good-bye, and I drove back to the hotel to see Joan and break the news to her.

Joan and I have been married twenty-two years now. We got married when I was an intern at Bellevue, on November 28 or 29, 1953—I can never remember which. We've had our problems and our fights—what couple married that long

49

hasn't?—but we've always gotten along reasonably well and I know I can say, and I hope and expect she'd agree, we love each other. (And don't ask me to explain what that means; you either know or you don't.)

We've got those six kids I've already mentioned and we lost a seventh about six hours after he was born. Generally we've had a wonderful life together.

We, like most people with or without children, have often said to ourselves, "We're too lucky. Things just can't go on this well. Sometime we've got to get a bad break." As I drove back to the hotel all I could think was, *Well, it finally arrived, the bad break we've been expecting.*

It was twelve thirty when I got to the hotel and Joan was in the room. "How'd it go?" she asked.

"Not good," I said. "There's something the matter with my heart." That was all I needed to say. At that, I broke down. We put our arms around each other and I cried. I just let it all come out. I'd had a blow; it hurt and I couldn't keep my emotions under control any longer. The crying didn't last long; two, maybe three minutes and it was over. I sat down.

"I'm so sorry," Joan said.

"I know you are." I said. "So am I. But that doesn't change anything. No matter what happens now, our lives can never be quite the same again. It's the end of an era for us—a wonderful era, but it's over. We've got to start planning and living our lives differently. We've got a lot of responsibilities to our kids or at least we feel we do, and we've got to do what we can to prepare for them. I don't worry because I can't leave them lots of money but I do want them to have decent educations if they want them. And I want to protect you as much as I can. I'm going to keep hoping I'll be around another twenty years, but we've got to face the fact that it's possible I won't be. That's always been a possibility, of course; only now it suddenly looks more possible.

"Come on," I said, standing up, "What do you say we get out of here and get back to Litchfield? We can talk about it as we drive back and over the weekend at Telemark. But let's not let it spoil the weekend for us. We've been living well and having a pretty good time until now and nothing really changed this morning. We just got some information we didn't have before, some bad news we've got to live with."

"Listen," Joan said, "I know you're going to be okay. If God wanted you to die, He'd have let you die on that racquetball court. Because He didn't means He wants you to keep on going."

"You may have a point at that," I said. "It sounds reasonable to me."

While Joan packed the bags I called George Smith at Brooks. "George," I told him, "I'm sorry to bother you again, but as soon as you look at my stress EKG, if you see anything unusual will you call me?"

"Sure will, Bill," he said. "Have a good time at Telemark and try not to worry."

Joan and I picked up the bags and left. As we walked to the car I noticed a first subtle change in our relationship; not so subtle, really. Joan picked up the heavier suitcase and left the lighter one for me. When I tried to trade with her she wouldn't let me.

By such trivial signs are important events marked—or something.

51

Chapter VI

Oddly, at the time I'd failed my stress test, as Bill and I scheduled the angiogram neither of us mentioned the probability that I'd need to have a heart operation, specifically a coronary by-pass operation. Yet it was the by-pass operation that both of us were thinking about. Otherwise there wouldn't have been any point in doing the angiogram.

Until 1967 most doctors treated patients with coronary artery disease medically. For attacks of angina, nitroglycerine tablets could be used to help relax the coronary vessels and temporarily increase blood flow to the heart. Anticoagulants, blood-thinning medicines, were sometimes prescribed to interfere with clot formation and, hopefully, keep obstructions from developing in the coronary arteries. Digitalis could be used to strengthen the heartbeat and there are a number of drugs available to help keep the heart rhythm regular. By using these medicines, when indicated, and encouraging patients to live reasonably, doctors could often help their patients to live long, comfortable, productive lives. In 1975 good medical treatment is still a very effective way to manage many—possibly most—patients with coronary artery disease.

But medical management of coronary artery disease does not really restore adequate blood flow to the heart. What it does is to slow down—possibly stop—progression of the disease. A good medical doctor will also teach a patient how to live his life without putting excessive demands on his heart. Medical management does not make a sick heart well.

So for many years surgeons have been looking for a way to increase the circulation to the heart, to give the heart new blood vessels or to repair the old.

I remember, for example, in 1953 when I was applying for a surgical internship, I was interviewed by a chest surgeon who said to me, "Dr. Nolen, how would you treat a patient with angina?"

I started to outline the medical treatment—nitroglycerine, anticoagulants, exercise, and all the rest—but he quickly interrupted me. "No, no," he said, "not all that nonsense. Tell me what operations you might perform."

Prodded by his suggestion, I remembered there were several operations one might perform for the patient with angina. I spouted them out: thyroidectomy (to slow down the body's metabolism), sympathectomy (cutting the nerves over which heart pain is relayed to the brain); and a wide variety of operations designed to increase blood flow to the heart (bringing the omentum, the so-called fatty apron up from the abdomen through the diaphragm and laying it against the heart, sewing a patch of lung to the heart, or even—so help me—sprinkling talcum powder on the heart in the hope that the irritation would stimulate the growth of new blood vessels).

When I'd finished reciting, the examiner said, "Great, Nolen, great! We'll have you thinking like a surgeon yet."

In 1975 we know that none of these operations were really any good. Admittedly, about 30 percent of patients swore they were "better" after their operations, whichever one it might have been; but 30 percent of patients will think they are improved, no matter what you do to them. This is what is known as the placebo effect. Convince patients that something will reduce their symptoms, and in patients susceptible to suggestion, the symptoms will be relieved, or ignored. Surgery can be used as a placebo just as sugar pills sometimes are.

The trouble with all these operations was that none of them really increased the blood flow through the coronary arteries. Before an operation could be developed that attacked the problem directly, two advances were necessary. First, surgeons had to be able to see where the coronary arteries were blocked, and second, they had to be able to operate on a resting heart.

The second of these goals was achieved first. Surgeons, engineers, and other scientists had been working for years to develop a heart-lung machine that could substitute for the heart while the surgeon stopped, opened, and operated on the heart. By 1954 such a machine had been built and surgeons were learning to use it effectively.

In 1959 the first goal was achieved. Dr. Mason Sones at the Cleveland Clinic in Ohio developed a technique in which a catheter (a hollow plastic tube) was inserted into an artery in the arm and then under x-ray visualization, threaded up the artery to the heart. The tip of the catheter could then be worked into the mouths of the coronary arteries. The physician would then inject dye into each of the coronary arteries and x-ray pictures could be taken that would show the inside of the arteries. Any blocks that existed could be clearly seen.

As heart-lung machines improved and physicians became more adept at performing angiography, surgeons worked to develop an operation that would restore blood flow directly to the coronary arteries.

Logically, one would think that the best approach would be to simply open up the coronary artery, remove the arteriosclerotic plaque that was causing the obstruction, and close the artery again. This approach was, in fact, tried, but it didn't work.

Remember, the left and right coronary arteries measure a little less than the size of a drinking straw in diameter at their origins, which are their widest parts. As they extend out into the heart, they become progressively more narrow. When surgeons opened these small vessels, removed the obstructing plaques, and closed the incisions with sutures, they couldn't help but narrow the vessel slightly, no matter how fine the sutures or how delicate the surgeon.

In addition, the wall of the artery from which the plaque was removed was left rough and irregular. This rough, narrow spot was an ideal place for clots to form; and, in fact, that is what often happened. The surgeon would remove the plaque or plaques from the coronary arteries, and a few hours or days later, clots would form, often completely blocking an artery that had been only partially blocked before the operation.

Finally, in 1967, a surgeon at the Cleveland Clinic, Dr. Rene Favaloro, hit upon the idea of by-passing the blocked area in a coronary artery. Instead of attacking the blocked area directly he took a vein from the patient's leg, sewed one end of it to the aorta—the biggest blood vessel in the body, the artery through which most of the blood to the rest of the body leaves the heart—and then sewed the other vein to the coronary artery, just beyond the point where the arteriosclerotic block lay. If there were two blocks, he used two strips of vein. Soon Dr. Favaloro, and other heart surgeons, were using as many as four strips of vein to by-pass blocked coronary arteries. Some surgeons also began to use an internal mammary artery, an artery that lies just behind the sternum, as a by-pass. This artery, which originates from a branch of the aorta, was ideally located for use as a by-pass, and had the added advantage of being a so-called living graft, since it remained attached to its parent vessel at one end.

As experience accumulated it became evident to all but the most skeptical physicians that the by-pass operation had merit. After the operations, when patients were back to full activity, about 90 percent of patients who had had a by-pass operation reported that they were free of angina. This was a much larger group than one would expect from a simple placebo effect.

Moreover, when angiograms were done a year or two after the operations, it was generally found that in those patients whose symptoms had disappeared the grafts were still open; in those whose symptoms had returned, the grafts had become obstructed, presumably with blood clots. This proved rather convincingly that it was the by-pass itself, not a placebo effect, that made patients well.

At first, as is generally the case when a new operation is developed, the mortality rate was relatively high: 10 to 20 percent in some hospitals. However, as surgeons, anesthesiologists, and the technicians who ran the heart-lung machine got more experience, mortality rates dropped rapidly. By 1975 many hospitals were reporting mortality rates of less than 1 percent, about as low as the mortality associated with appendectomy.

I was certainly glad, as I contemplated the possibility that I might undergo a by-pass operation, that the operation had come as far as it had.

CHAPTER VII

June 20, 1975–June 24, 1975

Joan and I had a wonderful time at Telemark even though, in quiet moments, we couldn't help but reflect on what was facing us on our return to Minneapolis.

I swam and played golf, though I have to admit we rented a cart and I walked only half the holes; the course at Telemark is a beautiful but rather hilly one, cut right out of woods. We even played doubles in tennis. My son Bill teaches tennis at Telemark in the summer so he arranged the match, and he took it easy on me. When he plays as well as he can, he always beats me six to zero, six to zero.

We danced and drank and partied at night and slept late in the morning. We had, as I've said, a marvelous time, and not once did I have that strange burning sensation. I suppose I didn't push myself beyond the point where, almost subconsciously, I knew I might have trouble.

I did, though, have some strange, unexplainable twinges of soreness and pain in my chest and shoulder; and this brings us to an important point. Angina is a symptom, something you experience but can't see. You don't turn red or white or blue when you're having angina. There's no physical evidence that you're in trouble.

So, of course, as soon as the label "angina patient" has been painted on you, your mind begins to play tricks. You become aware of minor symptoms you'd have previously ignored without a second thought. You read into innocuous twinges intimations of death. Dozens of times over the weekend I had to fight these fears off, saying to myself in effect, "Come on, Nolen—be a big boy. Don't let every little shadow frighten you." But that was easier said than done.

I had one method that I could sometimes use to reassure myself that I wasn't going to keel over with a heart attack. Bill Petersen had told me that my symptoms and signs during the stress test first appeared when my pulse reached 122. So, whenever I was apprehensive, I'd check my pulse; if it was below 122, I'd relax. I knew this wasn't a foolproof system; the arterial block, or blocks, that presumably had caused my pain might be progressing so that less exertion would produce symptoms, but I thought this was hardly likely.

During quiet moments, resting after lunch or having drinks before dinner, Joan and I would talk about the possibilities. She was the eternal optimist. "I just bet that angiogram will be one of those 10 percent that are normal," she'd say, but, much as I'd like to have agreed with her, I was as certain as I could be that wouldn't be the case. So I insisted we talk over some practical matters. What she should sell and what she should hang onto; how she should try to educate the children; whose advice she ought to seek and take as far as financial matters went. I had a will and a sort of trust setup through a bank but, of course, neither Joan nor I really understood it. And, of course, it wouldn't have enough money in it if I died at forty-seven to provide even reasonably well for a wife and six children over a long period. I've made a fairly decent income over the last few years but I'm a long way from being what anyone could even remotely label a "rich man."

Two things entered my mind (and I assume Joan's) that neither of us ever brought up. One was where she would live if I died (i.e., stay in Minnesota or go back to where our relatives live in Massachusetts) and the second was where she would bury me if I died. Our son who died just after birth is buried in Litchfield; all the others of our families who have died are buried in Massachusetts. I guess there are things that are just too sensitive for people—at least people like Joan and me—to discuss, even though, from the practical view, they should be talked about. (We still haven't discussed them, so I guess we have a tacit agreement that the survivor will make those decisions on her or his own.)

Inevitably, Monday rolled around and we had to drive back to Litchfield. Mary (our thirteen-year-old) had come with us; the rest of the kids had elected to stay home, either because their summer jobs made that necessary or because they wanted to be with their friends.

Joan and I had talked a little about how much to tell our

children and how to tell it to them. We had decided that getting them all together (which would have been a difficult job in itself) and breaking the news might make too big a thing of the operation.

Besides, they were individuals of different ages and attitudes; some would probably want to know more and some would need to know less than the others.

So I told them each individually what was going to be done. I didn't go into any great detail. Basically, varying the words and details with each one, I explained that I needed to have some special x-rays done and that after that I might need a heart operation. I told them that the arteries to my heart were probably blocked and that the operation would remedy the problem.

I was prepared for a few questions, but none of the children asked any. I assume they all knew that I was going to have a major procedure that would involve a risk to my life, but—and, of course, this is generally true of the young—they assumed everything would go all right, just as youngsters in their twenties go to war and assume they'll be among the survivors, while those of us on the far side of forty assume that if anyone's going to be shot it will be us. At any rate, we told them all, and though I'm sure they were concerned, they weren't really frightened, which we felt was as it should be.

When we got back to Litchfield on Monday evening I called Dr. Smith at his home to find out if he wanted me to be fasting when I arrived at Brooks.

"That won't be necessary," he said. "Any fasting tests we may need we can get later. Just try to get in by noon."

Bill hadn't told me anything about what to expect when I went to the hospital for my angiogram. He assumed, and he was right, that I knew what would be done to me and what risks were associated with the procedure.

Generally, this is an unwise policy. A doctor is well advised to assume that the patient knows nothing of what will happen to him or her once they've stepped inside the hospital doors. Usually, such an assumption is correct.

I have a two-word rule that I follow when I'm preparing a patient for surgery: no surprises. Too often surgeons forget that going through an operation is a new and frightening experience for the patient. This may be the hundredth time the surgeon has taken out a gallbladder, but it's the first time the patient has had hers removed.

Before the patient goes into the hospital, I sit down with her and explain exactly what is going to happen. I tell her about the sleeping pill she'll get in the evening, the shaving that will be necessary, the enema she'll have to have. I tell her about the injection she'll get preoperatively that will make her drowsy and her mouth dry; about the needle that will be put into her vein in the operating room; about what it will be like to wake up in the recovery room. I warn her about the discomfort she'll have postoperatively and about the painkillers that will be available to alleviate her distress. I try to anticipate everything that will be done to her and for her so that she won't be frightened by the unexpected. Mental preparation for an operation is at least as important as physical preparation.

Try as I may not to leave anything out, I have to confess that occasionally I slip up. One such occasion stands out very clearly in my mind, since it involved the wife of a physician friend; in medical circles we say that if anything can ever go wrong, it will go wrong when the doctor is caring for a nurse, a physician, or a member of a physician's family. I suppose that isn't statistically true, but it certainly seems as if it were true.

My patient—I'll call her Georgia—was a woman seventy years old, who had gallstones that were causing a lot of trouble. I planned to take out her gallbladder, and even though I knew she was a physician's wife and might know something of what to expect in the hospital, I still went over the entire routine with her in great detail—enema, shave, everything.

The operation went smoothly and, of course, I was pleased and assumed she would be, too. Instead, when I went to see her the morning after surgery, she seemed quite upset. I know her well, so after I'd told her how well she was doing I said, "Come on, now, Georgia, something's bothering you. Tell me what it is."

"All right, Bill," she said. "I wasn't going to say anything but as long as you've asked I will. I don't want you to think I'm not grateful to you for doing such a fine job with my surgery. I am. But I'm mad, too, because yesterday morning before I went into the operating room the nurse made me take my teeth out. I'll never be able to face Dr. Darcy [the anesthesiologist] again."

You just can't win them all.

Tuesday, June 24, was a real scorcher with temperatures in the high eighties. Joan drove in with me; she planned to spend a couple of nights at a motel, since we expected to drive back to Litchfield on Thursday. Our schedule, as arranged by Dr. Smith prior to entering Brooks, was: (1) admission and general physical examination on Tuesday (I had brought recent chest x-rays down on my visit to Bill Petersen a week earlier, and, of course, Dr. Smith had had my stress EKG for the last six days so not much of a preliminary workup would be necessary); (2) angiogram on Wednesday morning at 9 A.M.; (3) observation overnight, to be sure there were no complications; e.g., bleeding from or development of clot in the artery through which the angiogram was done; (4) discharge at noon on Thursday, when Joan and I would drive back to Litchfield. Dr. Smith had suggested that I not play tennis for a couple of days after the angiogram, but he thought it would be all right if I went back to operating. In fact, I had two patients with gall bladder disease scheduled for operation on Friday.

Then, depending on what the angiogram revealed, Joan and I would decide where to go if it was apparent that an operation was either necessary or advisable. I'd tentatively decided I'd ask Frank Johnson to do it, but I was still considering the possibility of going to another surgeon—Effler in Cleveland or Cooley in Houston, for example—someone who did the operation at least once and often several times a day. But that decision we'd make at leisure after the angiogram, or so we thought.

I was admitted to a very nice room at Brooks. It was in a newly remodeled section of the hospital, and it was designed for heart patients who needed close supervision, but not quite as intense supervision as was necessary in the first day or so after a heart operation. The nurse was pleasant and efficient. She showed me how to work all the buttons that raised and lowered the bed, turned on the television, or called the nurse; and she told me, "No, it won't be necessary to get into your pajamas yet. Just make yourself comfortable."

During the next couple of hours Joan and I sat, talked, and read the books we'd brought. Once we were interrupted when a laboratory technician came in to take some blood samples, and a little later the technician who would be assisting Dr. Smith while he did the angiogram came in and explained the procedure to me.

"There's nothing to be afraid of," he reassured me. "We do two or three a day and haven't had any trouble for as long as I can remember. The important thing to remember is to cough hard when we ask you to; that helps get the dye out of the coronary arteries. About the only possible risk is during those few seconds when the dye is in the arteries. Sometimes the dye causes an irregular heartbeat." I knew most of this, but was happy to have it explained to me again.

Finally, at 4 P.M. Dr. Smith came into my room. We shook hands and I introduced Joan to him. He had my stress EKG in his hands, and he sat down on the side of my bed.

"Frankly," he said, "I don't like the looks of this EKG. It's impossible to say with certainty—I could be wrong— but most of the time when we see a pattern like the one here it means three-vessel disease. If that is the case, then we generally like to proceed with surgery soon after the angiogram. We might wait till the next day, but sometimes we take the patient directly from the angiogram room to the operating room. I think before we proceed with the angio we'd better have a surgeon in to see you so he'll be on call in the morning. Whom would you like me to call?"

I don't know how I looked at that moment, but I know how I felt—as if I'd just been unexpectedly handed a notice informing me that I was tentatively scheduled for execution in the morning. A reprieve was, of course, possible but highly unlikely.

When I'd had a little time to absorb what Dr. Smith had

said, and he had said it all very clearly, I looked over at Joan and could see that she was absolutely terrified. I was pretty terrified myself. I said, "You mean that when I have the angio tomorrow there's a possibility I may have to have the operation immediately thereafter?"

"That's right," Dr. Smith said. "I don't want to frighten you (as if he hadn't already), the chance may be only five or ten percent. But, on the strength of this EKG I think the chance is a real one. I don't want to go in there unprepared, and [in a comradely tone] I'm sure you don't, either."

"Agreed," I said. "But you have to realize I wasn't prepared for this. I haven't really made up my mind whether I want the surgery done here or somewhere else. If I'd known that I had to make that decision, I'd have made it, of course, but I might not be in here right now. You are telling me, aren't you, that if I'm not ready to go ahead and be operated on here then I'd better not have the angio done here tomorrow?"

"That's right," he said.

"Why didn't you call me and let me know the situation before I came down here?"

"I guess I was a little remiss there," he said, sounding not at all apologetic. "I didn't get around to looking at the stress EKG until this afternoon."

"Oh," I said. "Well, I hope you'll understand that this comes as sort of a shock to me—and to Joan. Can you give me a few minutes to make up my mind. And can I use the phone?"

"Sure," he said. "I'll be out at the nurse's station. Let me know what you decide."

When Dr. Smith had left the room I said to Joan, "What do you think?"

"I don't know what to think," she said. "It's such a shock. All I know is I'm scared to death."

I was recovering from this new blow and was beginning to get angry. "I'm going to make a few phone calls."

First, I called Bill Petersen at his office and told him what had happened. "God, Bill," he said, "I'm sorry as hell. I reminded George about that EKG twice, the last time just three days ago."

"I haven't made up my mind what I'm going to do yet. I hope you won't be hurt if I leave?"

"Not at all," he said. "You do whatever you think is right. I'm just sorry about the screw-up."

Next I called a surgeon friend of mine who practiced at Abbott and Brooks. I told him what had happened. "What would you do?" I asked.

"Tough question, Bill," he said. "I like the guys who are doing the heart work there and they do a good job. But I guess, if you want my opinion, if it were me I'd go someplace where they're doing open-heart work every day."

Finally I called Chappie Thayer, a surgeon in Portsmouth, New Hampshire.

You know how if you use the word "friend" loosely, most of us can claim dozens or hundreds, but if you put it in capitals—restrict it in that exclusive, indefinable way—you have, if you're lucky, two or three. Well, Chappy is one of my FRIENDS, capitals all the way.

We met in 1949 when we were both freshmen in medical school. We don't see each other as often as we like, but we're in touch by phone at least once a month. If I have a problem—surgical, financial, family—the first guy I call is Chappie. And I think he does the same with me.

I've often used him as a long-distance consultant. I have

family and friends in New England who, when they run into some unusual medical problem, call me and ask whom I'd recommend. I, in turn, call Chappie, since being in practice close to Boston and having trained at University Hospital there, he knows who is who in the New England area. If he doesn't know what dermatologist is an expert in acne, he knows someone who does. And somehow, every time he's helped me refer a friend to a physician, the friend not only gets good medical care but good personal treatment as well; and, as we all know, the two don't always come together.

I caught Chappie just as he was leaving his office. My voice started to crack—this sudden blow had shaken me emotionally—but I finally got it under control. Before I could say anything Chappie said, "It's not Joan, is it? She doesn't think you've got some other woman, does she?" He was serious, but he also relieved the tension. I was able to switch from tears to laughter. "No," I said, "not that. Something different. Worse or better, I suppose, depending on how you look at it."

I explained exactly what had happened. "I was going to call you before I decided on surgery," I said, "but I didn't think there was any rush. I thought I'd wait until after the angio. Now," I continued, "I'm too emotionally involved to make a reasonable decision. What do you think I ought to do?"

"I'll tell you what to do," Chap said. "You get out of that hospital as quick as you can. Go on home. You need a day or two to pull yourself together. It's too late now, but tomorrow I'll start phoning around. I know they're doing a lot of by-passes at the General (Massachusetts General Hospital) and George Battit is sort of the head anesthesiologist in the heart surgery unit. George is a good friend of mine. I'll phone him and then call you back tomorrow or Thursday. But, for now, get out of that place. If you don't I'll come out and drag you out."

"Okay, Chap," I said. "I really appreciate your help. I'd about decided to leave, anyway, but I needed reassurance. I'll be out at the lake tomorrow; you can reach me there."

"Fine," he said, "It will probably be late in the afternoon. Give my love to Joan."

"And mine to Betty," I said. And I hung up.

I got off the bed and asked Dr. Smith, who was just outside waiting for me to finish my calls, to come back to the room.

"George," I said, "I hope you won't take this personally—it's no reflection on you, the hospital, or the surgeons who work here—but I'm leaving. I'm just not mentally ready to sign up for an operation here or anywhere else so I'm going home. I'll let you know, directly or through Bill Petersen, when I've reached a decision. Sorry to screw up your schedule."

"Don't worry about that," George said. "You do whatever you think is right. I'm sorry about the misunderstanding. I'm afraid I was a little remiss."

I felt like saying, "You're (damn) right you were," but I didn't. I let it drop.

Joan and I picked up our few things, went down and got into the car, and drove back to Litchfield. "Well," I said, once we were in the car, "what do you think?"

"Now that I'm over the shock, there isn't any question—I'm glad we left."

"That stress EKG had been sitting down there six days. I'd reminded him of it twice and so had Bill Petersen. I like and trust Frank Johnson, but I'm not having any heart operation in a place where the cardiologist pulls something like that. I don't expect extra-special treatment, but I do expect reasonable, intelligent careful treatment, and as far as I'm concerned, Smith struck out. I know he's a smart cardiologist and maybe this is the one time in a hundred or a thousand that he screwed up but it's once too much for me. I'm going home and take a couple of days off—I haven't got any surgery scheduled until Friday, anyway—and make up my mind what to do. But I've made one definite decision already, I'm not going back to Smith.''

"You know," I added, "I wonder if I weren't a doctor how I'd have reacted? Would I have gone ahead and picked a surgeon; or, more likely, let Smith pick one for me? Would I have had the angio and the operation, even though I had misgivings?''

"I think you would have," Joan said. "I'm almost certain I would. It's so hard to question a doctor.''

"I agree," I said. "Here I am a surgeon, with a reasonably complete knowledge of what by-passes are all about, and I almost went along with him. Sometimes I think all doctors, and I include myself, don't realize what authoritative figures we are. We take our power for granted, and we shouldn't.''

"Well, you're out and away for now," Joan said. "Let's not worry about what's to come till tomorrow.''

Now that the whole experience is behind me, I feel guilty about criticizing Dr. Smith in print. I suppose my reluctance stems from the camaraderie of the medical profession that makes us hesitant about censuring one another. We deal in uncertainty. There isn't a physician alive who hasn't, at least once, been guilty of an error in judgment. Any honest physician will admit that he can remember cases in which one or more of the decisions he made proved in retrospect to be wrong, and as a result of his misjudgment the patient suffered. Sadly, physicians are not omniscient.

But honest errors in judgment—mistakes—are one thing; they hurt, but a reasonable patient will forgive them. Errors in management that occur because a doctor neglects to do his job are another matter. I feel no obligation to forgive the doctor guilty of that sort of practice.

Unfortunately, it happens only too often. I'm sure I've been guilty as often as has Dr. Smith or any other physician. We get caught up in the science of medicine. We worry about selecting the proper pills, choosing the best operation, ordering the appropriate x-rays; and we neglect the art of medicine. We forget that we are not dealing solely with an abstract scientific problem, but rather are treating a human being—one who is, in all probability, extremely apprehensive, frightened of what he or she may have to face. Too often we doctors do our jobs as scientists but fail as humanists.

This is where Dr. Smith had erred. I had no grounds for criticizing his technical work. In all probability he had interpreted my electrocardiogram properly and, I feel sure, if I had stayed at Brooks he would have done the angiogram capably, and would then have made a sound recommendation for or against an operation. He hadn't been guilty of malpractice in any legal way.

But, he had known that I, like any other prospective heart surgery patient, was apprehensive. He had known that I was very concerned about the interpretation of my electrocardiogram. And yet, though the electrocardiogram had been available to him for six days, he had failed to spend the thirty seconds it took him to interpret it until I was in the hospital being prepared for an angiogram. I'd never get a judgment against Dr. Smith in a court of law, but nevertheless he was guilty of malpractice.

(As a physician, I'm reluctant to criticize Dr. Smith, but as a patient, I shall let the criticism stand.)

Chapter VIII

June 25, 1975–June 27, 1975

Wednesday and Thursday, Joan and I stayed at our lake place. Mary was in and out, depending on her summer recreation program activities. Annie was teaching tennis in the summer program; Jim and Julius were working, laying sod; and Jody was back in Massachusetts where she had a job as a chambermaid at a resort on the Cape.

I kept busy in the mornings working on two columns for McCall's. I knew that if I had to have a heart operation—and at this point we'd both accepted the idea as almost a certainty—I probably wouldn't be up to writing a column for the next month.

Afternoons Joan and I played nine holes of golf each day.

I walked the nine holes and didn't have any trouble, but the Litchfield Golf Course is one of the flattest you're ever likely to see. I swam at least once a day. I didn't try playing either racquetball or tennis.

Friday I went to the hospital in the morning and did the two gallbladder cases that I had previously scheduled, but I didn't go to the office in the afternoon. I didn't want any more patient responsibility till I had resolved my own problems. It didn't seem fair to them for me to take on responsibility for their health when I was already concerned over my own.

The possibility that I might die—soon—had become very real. I knew the mortality for even a triple by-pass procedure was low—5 percent to 10 percent, in a good hospital—but, as John D. Mountain, M.D., an instructor during my days as a surgical resident, used to say, "Always remember, Nolen, statistics are fine, but it's one hundred percent for the guy that's got it." If I were part of the 5 percent mortality, I'd be 100 percent dead.

Surgeons by the nature of their work see a lot of death. Sometimes it's sudden and unexpected, as when a seventeen-year-old kid drives his car head-on into a tree; sometimes it can be anticipated, as in the eighty-five-year-old man with disseminated cancer. For me, certainly, dealing with death has always been difficult, one of the necessary jobs that I liked least in my surgical practice.

I told Joan several times over these few days something that I've been telling her off and on for years: "If something should happen, and I don't make it, remember—I've had a wonderful time."

I mean it. I've seen too many people live for their retirement days only to be struck down by death or crippled so they couldn't get around when they finally reached that time in their life when they were finally "going to have fun" ever to postpone enjoying life today for what I might have tomorrow. Joan and I have tried to enjoy every day of our lives.

There have, of course, been practical restrictions. With six children, we've always had obligations that have prevented us from spending or traveling as freely as we might otherwise have done. But for these small sacrifices, we've had the joy—and it has been a joy—of having the six children. I know, I know, this isn't the way to think these days, and I don't expect my children will each have six children. But we had them before almost anyone was aware that a dangerous population explosion was upon us. And since Joan really doesn't care anything about mink or sable, and I look upon a car not as a joy but as a necessary evil, our tastes are relatively simple. We still, for example, live in the house we bought when we moved to Litchfield. We paid $13,500 for it then (in 1960), and for that price the owners threw in half the furniture, which we still use. Joan often says, as does everyone else who sees it, that it doesn't look like a "doctor's house." But what do we care? It's comfortable and conveniently located so that the kids, as they've grown up, haven't needed us to chauffeur them around. What more could one ask of housing?

This next is going to sound egotistical, but it's a reflection of the way I think so I'll say it anyway. Some of us want a little piece of what passes, at least during their lifetime (and I realize this is a contradiction), for immortality. Mothers, I think, get this sort of satisfaction from the children they bear; fathers, too, but less so.

In my case I'd had a taste of fame and a crack at immortality in the success I'd had in writing. I knew that if I died the books I'd written, whatever their merit (something I'd prefer not to discuss here) would still exist. Hopefully, for a few years more at least, they might entertain—possibly influence other people. So, in a sense, even though I were dead I wouldn't be dead. And this was consoling to me. I realize that other men and women probably have done other things that they feel will survive them, and take satisfaction from that. Here, I can only speak for myself.

In fact, I've sometimes asked myself, "Bill, if you could have made a deal with God in which you'd agree not to write any books in exchange for an extra ten years of life, would you have done it?" I'm glad that offer hasn't and won't be made, but I think if it were I'd pass up the extra ten years. But I'm forty-seven. If I were Keats who died at twenty-six, and the deal was no poems in exchange for an additional forty years, would I make the deal? Tough question.

I've often wondered what Jack Kennedy would have done had he been offered a deal by God: "Look, Jack, you don't get elected President and I'll let you live till seventy." I think he'd have chosen to be President, but who knows?

One more of these philosophical digressions: On Friday, after I finished operating, I came out to the lake at noon, planning to relax till I met Joan in town at three.

Before I had angina, before I was so concerned with death, I always enjoyed these two-hour lunch breaks. If I weren't playing tennis I'd come out to the lake by myself, sit in the sun, read the paper, take a nap, then a quick swim, and go back to town. I enjoyed being alone for a couple of hours.

This Friday I got as far as the nap and had to leave. I

78

hated being alone. With death hovering so near (or so it seemed), I wanted to be with my family. I wanted them all around me. It seemed to me, that Friday afternoon, that I could even understand how someone, faced with imminent death, might take his whole family and shoot them and himself. Just to keep them all together. A horrible thought— and I'm glad I'm rid of it—but it did enter my mind.

Just as I could now understand how a friend of mine, living with angina, in constant fear of death, had taken a gun and killed himself. I'm sure he had finally decided that he simply could not live with the fear of death. He'd rather die and be done with it. I hadn't understood it at the time it happened, but I did now.

So I stopped trying to take a nap and got up and drove into town.

A fairly large part of these three days was spent trying to decide where to go for the angiogram and, if necessary, the surgery.

I've often been asked, "How do you pick a good doctor?" and I've answered—sort of flippantly, I guess—"Just look around for a friend who seems to be in good health, find out how he or she likes their doctor, and go to him." And actually, with some qualifications (make certain the physician is an M.D. with a valid license, preferably on the staff of an accredited hospital), it isn't a bad answer.

But this was different—mostly, I suppose, because I was the patient. And you have to realize that though in many ways it's helpful to be a physician when you're looking for medical care, in other ways it's difficult. It would, for example, be virtually impossible for me to have blind faith in any doctor.

Chappie called me, as promised, on Thursday. He told

me that George Battit had told him that the cardiac anesthesia at the Mass General was excellent. There were always two anesthesiologists on each open-heart case, and they were doing about five open hearts a day. George also told Chap that though they were all good, he'd make certain if I came there that the anesthesia team on my case would be the team he'd want if he were the patient. The quality of the anesthesia is just as important to the outcome of an open-heart case as the surgery; some might say, more important.

Chappie had also tried to call a friend of his who was one of the staff heart surgeons, but this individual was on vacation so Chappie had spoken to another surgeon named Eldredth Mundth. "He sounds great to me," Chappie said. "He's obviously knowledgeable, pleasant to talk to, and he's personally doing three cases a day. I checked back with George Battit and George says he's excellent. I told Mundth you'd probably call and he said he'd be glad to take care of you."

I thanked Chappie and then, as usual, talked it over with Joan. "The only problem," I said, "is that it's back in Massachusetts. It really would be easier to stay in Minnesota. Maybe I ought to go to the Mayo Clinic?"

"That would be easier," Joan said, "but don't let distance make a difference. I'm perfectly happy to go back to Massachusetts."

I called Dr. Mundth, talked with him, and even asked what he thought of Mayo's. "They do excellent work," he said. "I'm sure you'd be in good hands. And if you decide to come here, I'll be glad to see you."

"I'll get back to you," I said.

I then called a general surgeon I knew at the Mayo Clinic.

He was on vacation, so I asked to speak to one of the heart surgeons. I got the surgeon's secretary, identified myself, and explained my problem. "We'd be glad to give you an appointment," she said. "You could come on July second, but that will run us into the weekend of the fourth. It would probably be better if you came in the ninth. I'll put you down tentatively for an angiogram on the eleventh and save operating time for you on the fifteenth. How will that be?" Apparently I wasn't to get to talk with any doctor.

"Fine, I guess."

"Then we'll send a confirmation out to you today, together with a list of the nearby hotels and motels. The Kohler Hotel is probably most convenient, but you can look at price schedules and decide. Now, can I have your address?"

I gave it to her and hung up. When all the data arrived the next day, included in the big envelope was a card with a little space I could mark, saying, as I recall, "I will not be able to keep my appointment." I marked that with a big X and sent it back.

Let me make it perfectly clear: I know many of the physicians at the Mayo Clinic and without exception they are pleasant, friendly, and, above all, capable physicians. The surgical and medical work done at the Mayo Clinic is superb; the quality is excellent.

But, by the very nature of its size and the way it must necessarily function, the Mayo Clinic is an impersonal place. I send patients there frequently. Almost without exception they are very pleased with the care they received; also, almost without exception, they tell me, "I just wish I could have had it in Litchfield. Things are friendlier here."

I have never been a patient at the Mayo Clinic, and after

81

writing this, I probably will always be afraid to ever be one; though I don't say what I'm saying to be mean. It isn't only the lay people who call the Mayo Clinic impersonal; an ophthalmologist friend of mine, a well-known, highly respected physician from Boston, came to the Mayo Clinic because he was having some bizarre neurological complaints that required evaluation. "I'd been to the best neurologists in Boston, Bill," he said, "but I was so close to these people, working with them every day, that I thought their objectivity might not be as it should, so I went to Mayo's.

"They did an excellent job, as complete, efficient, and thorough an evaluation as I could possibly want. And I'm sure—and reassured—that they've made the correct diagnosis.

"But not once, in the three days I was there, did any one doctor sit down and talk, personally, one on one, with me. Five doctors made rounds on me every day—always in clumps. Great scientific medicine—but impersonal as hell."

The only other two places I seriously considered going were to Houston, where Denton Cooley, the fastest gun in the West (and, reportedly, an excellent technician) has his big heart hospital; or to the Cleveland Clinic, where by-pass surgery really came into its own and where the stars are (or were, till recently)—Dr. Effler, who has done thousands of by-passes with very low mortality rates, and Dr. Sones, who pioneered in the field of cardiac angiography. But I called friends of mine who were acquainted with both places. One said, "Bill, if you think the Mayo Clinic is impersonal, wait till you see Cooley's place in Houston. It makes the Mayo Clinic look like the warmest, most sociable place on earth." The friend who knew the Cleveland Clinic warned me off. "They're great," he said, "and they've got more experience than anyone. But there's a sort of academic upheaval going on and right now I'd stay away."

So I decided on Massachusetts General.

Let me admit that other factors entered into my decision. I had received my medical education at Tufts in Boston, so naturally I have always looked on Boston as a leading medical center, as it is generally acknowledged to be.

Although I'd only been to Mass General a few times as a student—it's a Harvard Medical School teaching hospital—I knew it had a reputation as one of the great, if not the greatest, hospitals in the world. At the General they provide care for the indigent as well as the wealthy; they carry on research in every department, though it's basically oriented toward patient care; and it is certainly one of the best of the teaching hospitals. An internship or residency at Massachusetts General Hospital is a prized possession, and, this if anything, was probably the most critical point in my decision.

I knew that staff doctors—fully trained practicing physicians—might do the definitive things to me, such as the angio and the actual suturing of the grafts. But I also knew that from ten at night till seven in the morning, the kind of care I got was going to depend on the quality of the nurses and residents that were in the hospital at the time. I knew that if I went to the Massachusetts General Hospital, I'd be assured of round-the-clock care by some of the best resident physicians in the country. With surgery—heart surgery particularly—the unpredictable experience it necessarily is, this could be critical.

Sure, I knew that medical students, interns, and residents would, under supervision, be providing some of my care.

That news didn't bother me; I welcomed it. I believe in teaching hospitals.

Let me say, quite clearly, that I am referring only to teaching hospitals that attract residents who are graduates of the medical schools of the United States, Canada, and Great Britain. I am talking specifically of teaching hospitals, associated with medical schools in the United States.

I would not want to be left alone—i.e., without a private physician of my own choosing—in a hospital where medical responsibility is handed out to graduates of medical schools from foreign countries where medical education is second-rate. Unfortunately, graduates of these second-rate schools can be found working in many of the hospitals in the United States.

I think, personally, that it's a shame that the United States, still one of the richest nations in the world, can't afford (or is unwilling) to produce all the physicians we need, particularly when thousands of well-motivated, well-qualified graduates of our own universities and colleges are rejected each year, simply because our medical schools haven't the space for them.

But as long as we continue to import about one-third of our physicians, and as long as I'm unable (with the exception I've mentioned) to differentiate the good imports from the bad, I'm staying out of hospitals where important medical decisions are left to doctors of questionable ability. Far, far better—I can't emphasize this enough—to have no house staff at all than to have a poor one. Where there is no house staff, there are usually well-trained nurses who can and will do a lot of the things a good resident physician might otherwise do; and, if necessary, she can call the private doctor in. That's a hell of a lot safer than having a poorly educated doctor, over here on some sort of limited license, making the decision that you need some powerful pill or perhaps even a quick operation. And if you don't think that happens, in hospitals with third-quality residents supervised only loosely by busy private doctors, you are very much mistaken.

As a general rule, even if you are reasonably certain that you're going to need an operation, it's best to have a medical doctor as the overall supervisor of your care. Surgeons, with very few exceptions, are not the individuals who take responsibility for a patient over a long period of time. A surgeon is called upon to take charge of a patient for a few days before an operation, during the operation, and for a week or ten days after an operation. Then he may see his patient at six weeks, six months, and possibly once a year for a while. Any problems that arise between scheduled visits to the surgeon and during the years after the surgeon's work is done are usually managed by a medical doctor.

For the patient with heart disease, the medical doctor may be a GP, an internist, or a cardiologist, i.e., an internist who specialized in heart disease. Once I'd had my operation and had gotten through the first two postoperative weeks, the surgeon's work was done. Whatever could have been achieved by an operation would have been achieved, and unless some other condition requiring surgery arose, there would be very little my surgeon would have to offer me.

On the other hand, despite the operation, my heart would not be a "normal" one. The disease—coronary artery arteriosclerosis—would still exist and might even progress. I needed someone who would examine me periodically, and if the need arose, prescribe whatever medicines were necessary to keep my blood pressure at relatively normal levels and my heart functioning as it should. This is the sort of work a medical doctor does.

Surgical treatment provides a quick cure for problems, or sometimes an unhappier resolution, i.e., death. In either case the surgeon–patient relationship is usually a brief one. Medical doctors often have a long-term relationship with their patients and usually patient and doctor get to know each other well.

For all the foregoing reasons a patient who is ill, even if he or she is almost certain the disease is going to require an operation (hemorrhoids, for example, or gallstones) ought to go first to a medical doctor. Let the medical doctor make the overall evaluation of your health needs and then, if necessary, refer you to a surgeon. The indirect approach to a surgeon is not only best for the patient, but most surgeons prefer to have their patients come to them by referral rather than directly. I certainly do.

So, before finally deciding on MGH, I made one last call—to Dr. William Maloney, former dean of Tufts Medical College and now working in the health field at Tufts University. I asked him, as a personal friend and an internist who knows the doctors around Boston, if he could refer me to a cardiologist at the MGH. I preferred—and it was the preferred if not obligatory policy—to enter the hospital as the patient of a medical doctor rather than a surgeon, particularly since it hadn't as yet been definitely established that I'd ever need an operation.

"Bill," I said when I finally got through to him and had explained the situation, "I'd really like to have God Himself taking care of me. Short of that, I want the best I can get."

86

The next day, through an indirect series of referrals that began with Dr. Maloney and which are too complicated to go into here, I eventually wound up calling Dr. Roman Desanctis at MGH. He was, at first, reluctant to take me on. "I've had a medical problem myself recently and I am trying to cut back just a little," he explained, but in the end he said yes. (I don't think Roman, when it comes to service, has any no's at all in him.) The hospital and the angio and the operating rooms were all overbooked but finally Roman worked it out so that if I were willing to come into the hospital on July 4, a Friday, I could be admitted. I agreed and the arrangements were made.

Finally, I was committed.

Let me now make a final quick review of why I finally wound up deciding on Massachusetts General Hospital.

It would obviously be wrong to say that when I needed expert medical and surgical care I chose Dr. Desanctis as my cardiologist, Dr. Mundth as my surgeon, and the Massachusetts General as my hospital. At the time I first discovered I was ill, I'd never heard of either Dr. Desanctis or Dr. Mundth. I had heard of Massachusetts General, I knew it had a reputation as a fine, even a great, hospital, but I certainly was not intimately acquainted with it.

My choice was in fact made by Dr. Chappie Thayer. He happened to be a friend of mine, but that wasn't really a critical point. I let Chappie decide who should take care of me and where, because I trusted him and knew he had my best interests at heart. I put my faith in one doctor and relied on his decision.

Basically, this is what anyone has to do—ought to do—when he has a medical problem. Turn to one physician you know and trust and let him make the decisions for you. He may not choose the same doctors or hospital that Chappie chose for me; unless you live around Boston it's highly unlikely that he will. But he will choose a cardiologist whose judgment he trusts, and the cardiologist will in turn choose a surgeon or a hospital he trusts. There are many excellent cardiologists, many expert cardiac surgeons, and many fine hospitals and clinics in the United States. At any of them you can get superb care. But if I, a surgeon, can't know the intimate details about each of these places, certainly the layman can't be expected to know them, either. Because I am a surgeon, because I had just done a lot of research on the coronary artery by-pass, I did a lot of thinking and probing of other possibilities before making a final choice; but, after all the procrastinating, I took Chappie's advice. The best advice I can give you, if you're ever in a similar spot, is to do as I did: find one physician you trust and let him make the decisions for you.

Is there an inconsistency here? If I had to trust Chappie to choose for me, how can I be trusted, as I often am, to make critical choices for other patients?

It's a matter of personal involvement. I can make choices for others because I am medically knowledgeable. When the case involves me, or my family, my judgment is not to be trusted. As has been said, so many times, "The doctor who takes care of himself has a fool for a patient."

Chapter IX

June 28, 1975—July 4, 1975

Once the decision had been made I managed to relax, not as completely as before "the troubles" (that's the Irish in me), of course, but reasonably well.

I agreed to work part-time, operating or assisting in the operating room as was necessary, which meant, as it turned out, that I operated every day. The last patient I operated on before leaving for Boston on July 3 was an eighty-year-old woman who had broken her left hip. I'd put an artificial hip in on the right side two years earlier and she had done very well, so she wanted me to do her left side now that it had become necessary, and I felt I owed it to her to agree. Again, everything went nicely.

(The practice of surgery is, as I've written at length elsewhere, a very rewarding one. It's nice to be able to help people, usually quickly and often completely, and to know that they're grateful to you for the help you've given them.)

Afternoons I'd read or play golf or just sit around the lake. It was during these leisure moments that I'd sometimes get depressed.

I remember thinking one day how much I'd like to live to see my kids grow up, marry (if they chose to), build their careers, have their children. I was almost in tears thinking how much I'd hate to miss all that.

Then I realized that I'd really never be ready for death, at least not as long as I felt well and had reasonable control of my faculties. If I lived to watch Mary grow up and marry and have children, then naturally I'd want to stay alive to watch my grandchildren grow up. Obviously, what I really wanted, again assuming I could stay in reasonably good health, was to live forever. And I knew, from having watched older patients face death, that when that time came, even if I weren't in reasonable health, I'd still probably want to go on living. Certainly, most patients I'd seen had held onto life with all their might, even when it seemed to most of us younger, healthier observers that their lives weren't worth clinging to.

I know there's a movement afoot to allow people to sign papers saying that if and when they lose control of their bowels, or speech, or become generally incapacitated that they be put gently to sleep. And I know there are a lot of healthy people almost eager to sign such papers. My guess is that when the time to be "put to sleep" comes, most of those same people, with the last bit of strength they have in them, will be fighting to get those papers back so they can tear them up.

By now most of the people in Litchfield knew I had some sort of health problem; news of that nature spreads fast in a small town. Some thought I'd had a heart attack, some thought I had a mysterious ailment, and some—my partners and friends in whom I'd confided—knew as much as I did about what was wrong with me. We were invited out to dinner most evenings and usually we accepted. Joan and I both needed the distractions.

We spent one evening with Iris and Jerry Gloege, two good friends of ours. Jerry is a very sharp accountant and businessman and he has served as sort of an unpaid financial adviser to me over the last five years, ever since I got into writing and my income became, if not always greater than it had been, more irregular. I told him where I was going, why, and that Joan and I would be gone, if things went well, for about three weeks. Someone would have to pay the bills and take care of any other fiscal matters that came up during that time and I asked Jerry to accept my power of attorney for that interval, which he agreed to do.

On Thursday, July 3, we flew to Boston. I'd told Joan once or twice that she really didn't have to come, that I could go through it alone, but she wouldn't hear of that arrangement. I'd actually made the suggestion just as a formality; I knew she'd want to come with me and I certainly wanted her there. I didn't want to face this ordeal alone.

We arrived in Boston about 7 P.M. and went to the Holiday Inn in the Government Center (not a place I'd generally stay in Boston, but suitable for this trip because it was only a block and a half from the Mass General). We checked into

91

the motel, then went right out and saw Woody Allen in *Love and Death.* (Joan and I both are film buffs, though I like Allen more than she does.) After the show we went to Chinatown and ate and then walked up Tremont Street to Beacon Hill and back to the motel. The walk was about a mile, I'd guess, and mostly uphill. I had a funny feeling in my throat by the time we'd reached the top of the hill and it crossed my mind that it might be angina, but I had now reached the stage where I had given up trying to evaluate "strange" sensations. Angina is a purely subjective symptom, and as I've noted before, once you've had it your mind can increase or decrease its intensity and frequency with ease.

At noon the next day we walked over to the General and I was admitted to a corner room in the Phillips House, the plushest (or at least the most expensive) of the various sections that comprise the hospital; there are twenty-one buildings that make up Mass General, and the hospital has over one thousand beds.

Let me make it clear that I do not consider myself even remotely an expert on Massachusetts General Hospital. I spent a total of nineteen days there: six in the Phillips House, two in the operating room and recovery room, and eleven on Baker 12, the floor where all heart surgery patients are sent to recuperate once they're able to leave the recovery room. The only other parts of the hospital I visited were the rooms where the pulmonary function tests were administered, the x-ray department, the catheterization laboratory, the gift shop, and the chapel.

The Phillips House is not air-conditioned—it reminded both Joan and me of a rather dilapidated but once very nice old hotel—but I had a corner room and there was a nice breeze when both windows were open. As soon as we had been led to the room and shown how to work the bed, I was asked to sign a form that said (I haven't a copy but remember the essentials) that I would be responsible for paying any cost of the room over and above what my insurance would allow. The cost of the room on July 4, 1975—it may, of course, have gone up since then—was $154 a day. I signed. I had already decided that this was one venture where I was going to spend what I had to spend to get the best medical care I could, and worry later about paying for it. I had to pay $154 to get into the MGH on July 4, because on July 4 the only empty rooms at the MGH were the $154 ones.

I suppose I should point out now that I realize—as I'm sure the reader has from the beginning—that the story of my experience as a patient cannot be classified as typical. To begin with, I'm a physician, and physicians, nurses, and their families are usually treated "differently" by their fellow workers in the field of medicine from other members of the general public. This is natural; we belong to the same big fraternity (or sorority) and we share a lot of its secrets. But let me also make it clear that "different" treatment is just that; it is not necessarily better and it may often be worse. Sometimes, because we don't want to hurt or bother our confreres, we skip tests or examinations that we shouldn't skip; this can be dangerous.

I was also not typical in that my yearly income is higher than that of the average American. I am not wealthy but, like most physicians, I earn an income that certainly puts me in the top 20 percent of the country. So I can afford to spend more money on my health than can many others.

Finally, I wasn't typical in that I am reasonably well

known among members of the medical profession as a writer as well as a doctor. I suspect that a lot of the people who helped take care of me at the General wondered if they might not wind up later in some magazine article or book I'd write, assuming I survived. So perhaps some of the treatment I received was predicated on that possibility.

However, in all the important ways, I was treated like a typical patient. At the General, when it came to actual care, it didn't matter whether you were the wealthiest patient in the Phillips House or the poorest indigent in the oldest ward in the hospital. Everyone had his angiogram done in the same laboratories by the same people; had his operation in the same operating rooms by the same anesthesiologist, nurses, and surgeon; was sent to the same recovery room immediately after surgery and to the same intensive care ward, Baker 12, for final recuperation. This policy may not be true in every hospital, but I'm sure it is the rule in most places, a fact patients may find difficult to believe. I am certain it is true at General.

I didn't really expect to meet Dr. Desanctis on that hot Fourth of July afternoon. I thought he'd be home or at some beach and that I'd get a preliminary examination by an intern, but as it turned out, Dr. Desanctis was on call that weekend (he and four other cardiologists who are full-time at the General rotate night and weekend call) and half an hour after we'd arrived he entered the room.

We introduced ourselves, he met Joan, and he suggested that we get on a first-name basis—Roman and Bill—immediately, which took the formality out of things.

Roman is about forty-five. He worked his way through college at the University of Arizona and then went on to Harvard Medical School, followed by residency training in internal medicine at Massachusetts General. With further specialization he became a cardiologist.

He has a medium build, with a dark complexion.* He's married and has four daughters. He used to put in an average of fifteen hours a day at the General, treating patients, teaching residents and students, doing research, and spending whatever time was necessary on administrative duties. "I've cut down to twelve hours a day over the last year or so," he told me, "mainly because I've been having some leg trouble for which we haven't yet come up with a diagnosis. On twelve hours a day, I feel as if I had all the time in the world on my hands."

I liked Roman immediately and so did Joan. He's the kind of person who, when he talks to you or listens to you, makes you feel immediately that he is sincerely interested. You can sense that he really cares about you. (Again, this is a quality, like love, that you can't really define. You have to sense it. Roman has it.)

He began by sitting relaxed in a chair, as if he had all day to spend with me, and saying, "Why don't you just go ahead and tell me your story? I'll ask questions later."

So I told him everything that had happened, beginning with my match with Dave Gabrielson and including my past medical history, with emphasis on my blood pressure problem.

In addition, I told him—since I knew it was important—something of my heredity. "My father died at fifty-eight," I said. "He'd had a rapid pulse all his life but he had never,

---

*I am not going to tell you how tall anyone in this book is, because I have developed a "thing" about height. We put far too much emphasis on it in our society. It really doesn't matter a damn whether a person is 4′ 10″, 5′ 10″, or 6′ 10″. Somehow we equate height and positive attributes, and I think to do so is utterly ridiculous.

as far as anyone knew, had a heart attack. He died during a nap one afternoon. There was an autopsy and apparently he died of heart failure.

"My uncle, his brother, died of heart failure at sixty. I've always known there was a fairly bad heart history on my father's side—though his father lived till seventy-two before dying of heart disease—but I've always consoled myself that I look like my mother physically, and she's bright, active, and healthy at seventy-five. She still bowls every winter, plays golf summers, and works at the library year round."

Roman listened to my story very patiently, asked a few questions about diabetes in the family, and then, while Joan waited in the hall, did a complete physical examination. Joan came back in, Roman looked over the stress EKG, which I had brought with me from Minnesota, and then talked with us.

"It certainly sounds as if you're having angina. Not typical angina, of course, but what we call an anginal equivalent. Some people get rather bizarre symptoms rather than the typical squeezing pain; your "burning sensation" is atypical, but not radically so and it's a good bet that it's an anginal equivalent.

"This other business, your ability to go back and play for an hour without symptoms after taking a three- or four-minute rest to get rid of the pain, that isn't really too unusual, either. [Bill Petersen had told me the same thing.] We call it 'walk-through' angina. We're not really certain how to explain it, but I suspect that what happens is this. You start to exercise, not enough blood gets to the heart muscle, and you have angina. Then, while you're taking a break, small arterial branches, your collateral circulation, begin to relax and when you resume play they're open and delivering enough blood to your heart to keep you pain-free.''

"What about my stress EKG?" I asked.

"There isn't any question that it's abnormal. However, I hesitate to read too many specifics into it. It does strongly suggest anterior vessel disease, however, but whether one, two, or three vessels are involved I think would be pure guesswork to say."

"You agree I need an angio?"

"Yes," Roman said. "I've set it up for eight Monday morning. Chip Gold will do it. He's done hundreds and he's very good. Ordinarily I wouldn't be concerned about who did it, but I asked Chip because I know it's early in July and I thought you might be concerned."

"I have to admit that thought had entered my mind," I said and we both laughed.

July 1 is, by tradition, the day all new interns start working in a hospital. On July 1 everyone on the house staff moves up one notch, taking on more senior responsibilities. So there's a risk early in July that you might get an intern who is trying for the first time to draw blood from anyone, or a resident who is doing his very first angiogram. Even though I knew, if this were the case, that a senior man would be in attendance, supervising and ready to take over if necessary, it was reassuring to me to know that a veteran angiogram expert was going to work on me.

"As you probably guessed, there won't be much doing over the weekend and we really can't make any further plans regarding surgery till the angio is done. I'd like you to sleep here tonight so that we can get some blood studies in the morning, but if you'd like to leave around noon on Saturday it shouldn't be necessary for you to be back till about four on Sunday. Theoretically, if you're gone and an emergency comes in we'd have to take your room away from you, if it were the only one available. But that's not likely to occur.''

"Fine," I said. "I think I'll take advantage of the opportunity to get out, rent a car, and drive up to Ware to see my mother, brother, and sister."

"Sounds good." Roman said. "Don't do anything too strenuous.''

"I won't," I said.

"How about you, Joan? Any questions?" Roman asked.

"None, I guess," Joan said. "I'm just glad we're here."

When Roman left I asked Joan what she thought of him. "Wonderful," she said. "You can't help but like and trust him. I'm so glad we came out here."

"So am I," I agreed. "I feel as if we're in the best of hands.''

CHAPTER X

July 5, 1975–July 7, 1975

On Saturday I left the hospital. The nurses knew I was leaving, but it was still unofficial; the room was left in my name, though available in an emergency. In other words, if no one else used it that Saturday night I'd be allowed to pay the $154 and the MGH would not have an officially empty room.

Ware, where my mother and brother live, is in central Massachusetts, and is in my opinion quite an attractive town with a population of about six thousand. I have two married sisters, Mary who is two years younger than I, and Judy who is ten years younger. Mary lives in Simsbury, Connecticut, and Judy had just moved to Wilbraham, Massachusetts, near Ware, so all my relatives live in that area. My mother, my brother Jim, and my sister Judy were all in Ware on Saturday afternoon when we arrived, and it was nice to see them all. I had told them about my problem, and they knew I was scheduled for angiography on Monday.

My brother Jim, who is forty-two and a lawyer, has been a representative in the Massachusetts state legislature for eighteen years. I also met for the first time my brother's fiancée, Kathy McNerney, whom I liked immediately. Jim and Kathy were planning to marry on July 19 (both for the first time) and I was supposed to be best man at the wedding. The final decision on my participation was being held in abeyance until I learned the results of my forthcoming angiogram. We watched the tennis, Jim and I went for a swim after he had finished playing, and later in the evening we all went out to dinner. It was a very pleasant Saturday. (Incidentally, since we hadn't checked out of the Holiday Inn in Boston, figuring that the trouble of doing so for just one night was more than it was worth, I wound up paying for a hospital room, a room at the Holiday Inn in Boston, and a room in the Ware Motel, all for that one evening. Fortunately, the Ware Motel is a real bargain, $11 a night, double occupancy, and very pleasant as well.)

As usual—and this had been the case in Litchfield, too—several of the people I talked to knew people who had had by-pass operations and were now "as good as new, even better." With the by-pass operation there is now growing up a body of success stories designed to encourage and raise the spirits of anyone who is facing the procedure; it's rather like it was and still is with people who have had infarcts (another name for an infarct is a coronary thrombosis or coronary, for short) who are continually regaled with reminders that both Eisenhower and Johnson had had heart attacks. LBJ's heart attack was quite extensive, and he had gone on to function, healthily if not always happily, in the biggest, toughest job of them all, the Presidency.

Let me say to those of you who are telling these stories to friends facing the operation that they are, in fact, helpful. I was always glad to hear another success story even though I, as a combination physician-patient, knew the odds fairly well. But the stories did help and I was always glad to hear them.

Actually, heart-wise, for years my hero has been Peter Sellers. He had such a bad heart attack in 1964 that his heart stopped and had to be shocked back to beating five times in the course of his hospitalization. He has gone on to continued great film success, almost invariably in roles that require at least a moderate amount of physical exertion.

But what I really admire about Sellers is his remarkable postcoronary sexual activity.

Sellers had married one starlet, Britt Ekland, shortly before he had his heart attack. Which naturally, at the time of his hospitalization caused some rather ribald comment in the press. Sellers was then thirty-eight. But after recovering from his attack, he stayed married to her for five years and when this marriage broke up, married a second starlet, Miranda Quarry, with no untoward consequences. And as recently as 1974 he reportedly carried on a vigorous affair with Liza Minnelli, than whom there are in my opinion— based solely on her films, unfortunately—few more torrid women.

Sellers has accomplished all this without the benefit of by-pass operations, which had not been developed at the time he had his coronary. Which goes to show that, if you're fortunate, you can recover from a severe attack without surgery and live a vigorous life thereafter.

Since I am now on the subject of sex let me confess that worries about sex as it related to my heart were of some importance to me. I like sex—one might even say I love it—I had no inclination at all to cut down on my sexual activity. Some scientist has actually worked out a formula that shows that sexual activity leading to and through climax requires the same amount of energy it would take to pump a bicycle at a rate of eight miles an hour. I expect that there are individuals who climax at four miles an hour, others who get to twelve; eight is, I think, an average. (Sometimes, it seems to me, I'm doing at least one hundred.) I had never had anything resembling angina during sex (unless I had failed to notice it, not an impossibility), but neither did I ever want to have to worry about having an infarct and an orgasm at the same time, though a case could be made that it might be a very nice way to go. At any rate, the desire to remain sexually active was certainly one of the reasons I wanted to explore so completely the possibility of surgical relief from angina.

Sunday we watched my brother play a semifinal match, and at noon we left for Boston. We stopped at one of the Howard Johnson restaurants on the Massachusetts Turnpike for lunch, and not for the first time but for the first time so emphatically, I noticed how difficult it was to find on the menu anything suitably safe to eat. I'll write later about diet and heart disease, but most of us know or suspect, because we've been bombarded with the information in newspapers and magazines, that food cooked in grease is really not food most likely to keep the coronary arteries young and healthy. And yet everywhere you go—fancy four-star restaurants or fast-food chains of the Howard Johnson variety—you are stuck with menus that contain almost exclusively foods that are supposed to be bad for the coronaries. I, of course, was much more conscious of it on that Sunday than I had been over the previous forty-seven plus years of my life, but it was so apparent that it really shocked me. There was really nothing on the menu I could comfortably order unless it was to special order a lettuce and tomato sandwich without mayonnaise, so I settled for iced tea. It isn't that good-tasting, healthy foods aren't available; it isn't that people wouldn't buy them if someone who owns a restaurant would sell them; they just aren't on the menu anywhere (obviously there are exceptions to this rule, but they are few and far between). I don't want to jump ahead, but I'll repeat that I've got a few notes later on dietary adjustments, painless ones, that I've made.

We were back in Boston in my room at the Phillips House by 3 P.M.

In most hospitals the weekend staff is only about half as large as it is on weekdays. This does not mean that patients get less attention, even though the staff-to-patient ratio is obviously reduced, because hospital activity decreases markedly on weekends. For example, only emergency laboratory and x-ray studies are done on weekends; the only operations performed are emergency operations; generally, only patients who need emergency care are admitted on Friday and Saturday. In fact, as I've already noted, the only reason I entered the hospital on a Friday, and the Fourth of July at that, was because that was the only day in that general time period when I could get a bed.

There are some economists and administrators who think that hospitals should function at full capacity, at their regular hectic pace, seven days a week; that it is a waste of valuable facilities to let them sit relatively idle for two days out of every seven. There are even a few hospitals where, recently, a full seven-day schedule has been put into effect on a trial basis.

I disagree with this point of view. I think that weekend slowdowns are not only permissible but necessary. These breaks give the staff on duty a chance to catch up on all those little things that go undone during the hectic weekday schedule, little things that can and must be ignored because of the critical and overwhelming demands of the regular schedule.

As for the patients, generally, I think that the weekend breaks are good for them, too. It gives them a chance to catch their breath, free of the routine bloodlettings, physiotherapeutic exercises, and x-ray studies that are part of their daily hospital life.

Weekend breaks are as important to the staff and patients of a hospital as they are to the people who work in a factory, a law firm, or anywhere else.

But now the weekend was about over and it was time for some of the staff to get to work on me.

Shortly after I got back, an intern and a medical student came in and, in turn, each took a history and gave me a complete physical examination. I was happy to cooperate. Interns and medical students, in their desire not to miss anything, sometimes pick up little bits of history or previously unobserved physical findings that the other senior doctors have missed. I know some patients who have been in teaching hospitals who resent being "guinea pigs" for the physician in training; I think these patients have the wrong attitude. They've been offered an opportunity for thorough care that other hospitals, nonteaching hospitals, simply can't give their patients.

About 9 P.M. Chip Gold, the cardiologist who was going to do the angio stopped in to talk to me and to explain what would be happening the next day. Chip is one of the most pleasant people I have ever met, friendly and reassuring. A cardiologist like Roman but, at least temporarily, making a subspecialty of angiography.

"Basically," Chip told me, "there are two popular techniques for doing angiograms. One, the kind you watched at Brooks in Minneapolis, is known as the Judkin technique. Under local anesthesia a large needle is inserted through the skin and into the femoral artery. Then a series of catheters are passed under fluoroscopy (x-ray visualization) up the femoral artery, into the aorta, and eventually into the coronary arteries and the left ventricle, which are visualized by injecting dye into them. This technique doesn't require any incision; the cardiologist simply feels the beat of the femoral artery through the skin (it's easily felt) and inserts the needle blindly. An experienced angiographer almost never has trouble getting the needle, and subsequently the catheters, into the artery. The Judkin technique is very popular.

"But," Chip continued, "I was trained in the Sones technique and I prefer it. With the Sones technique I'll make an incision under local anesthesia just at the bend of your elbow. I'll expose the brachial artery and vein and then I'll make a small incision in the artery. I'll run the angiographic catheter up through this incision into the aorta, again under fluoroscopy. Then, just as you saw done in the Judkin technique, I'll inject the coronary arteries and finally the left ventricle with dye, and we'll take moving-picture x-rays that will show the blocks, if any, in your coronaries. The films will also show how well your left ventricle contracts; i.e., how healthy the muscles are.

"Using the Sones technique, at least as we do it here at the General, since the brachial vein is also exposed in the incision, I'll run a pacemaker wire up through this vein into your heart. [A pacemaker is an electric device that can stimulate the heart and control the heart rate. Thousands of patients—Supreme Court Justice Douglas being one of the best known—have "permanent" pacemakers, with wires running to their heart, implanted beneath the skin of their chest walls. These pacemakers are designed for people who have either permanent or frequently recurring abnormalities of heart rhythm. I put quotes around permanent, because the batteries do have to be recharged at intervals. With the new ones, several years can go by between recharging.]

"This temporary pacemaker," Chip continued, "will be strictly a safety device. If any arrhythmia is precipitated by the angiogram, and we don't expect any, then the pacemaker can be turned on. And, because the pacemaker can be used, you won't have to worry about coughing to clear out your coronaries."

Personally, besides the advantage of having a pacemaker in place, I was glad that Chip planned to use the Sones technique on me. I have injected dye into a few femoral arteries in the course of my practice, trying to pinpoint the location of an obstructing clot in an artery, and I knew that it was possible for the operator—surgeon or cardiologist—to miss the canal in the artery and inject the dye into the arterial wall. I also knew that, occasionally, it was possible to knock an unseen arteriosclerotic plaque off the femoral artery wall, causing circulation problems in the lower leg. No matter how many advantages there are to the Judkin technique, and there are some, it remains what a surgeon would call a blind technique. The Sones technique is open, and speaking as a surgeon, I've always preferred open techniques to blind ones. I've got a scar I wouldn't have had if the Judkin technique had been used; that scar doesn't bother me at all.

I slept well after a mild sleeping pill and at 8 A.M. a stretcher was wheeled into my room and I was rolled to the angio room two buildings away. Joan planned to come to the hospital at 10 A.M., when it was expected that I'd be back in my room.

The three technicians who would be assisting Chip, taking x rays, injecting dyes, rotating the table, introduced themselves to me. They were very friendly. "This is a relaxed place," one of them said. "Anytime you have a question, just ask. Anytime you have a complaint, let us know. If you want to watch the pictures, you'll be able to see them on that x-ray screen up there," and he pointed to a televisionlike monitor in a corner of the room.

For some reason I didn't want to watch my own angio, afraid, I suppose, that I'd see or imagine that I'd seen a block or an arrhythmia. I didn't want to see either.

I was strapped onto a soft, hammocklike device that could be electronically tipped and tilted. Then Chip came in, we said hello, and he started to operate on my outstretched arm. He takes great pride in his surgical talents. I've noticed, and when I mentioned it Chip agreed, that most medical men who do a little surgery take particular pride in the quality of the work they do. And I'll confess that even though I'd had minimal sedation—twenty-five mg. of Benadryl, which is really only a small dose of a commonly used antihistamine—I experienced almost no discomfort as Chip worked. I could feel the catheter and pacemaker as they slid up inside the arteries and veins in my axilla (armpit) on their way to the aorta and the heart, but there was no pain. Nor was there any discomfort as the dye was injected into the arteries. Each time my position was shifted (the goal is to get as many views of the heart and its arteries as possible to make evaluations as thorough as they can be), Chip would briefly turn on the pacemaker to make certain that it worked with me in my new position, but I could never tell when the pacemaker was on and when my own intrinsic cardiac nervous system was running things. The only sensation I felt was a flush that ran from my head to my legs and around my rectum when, as the last part of the study, they injected a large bolus of dye into my left ventricle, which was in turn ejected by ventricular contraction into my general circulation. I was warned by Chip and the technicians that this would occur, and when, so it didn't come as a surprise and it was over in less than thirty seconds. In fact the entire study, including the time it took to wheel me to and from the angio lab, took only one and a half hours.

"We'll put you on the monitor for the first few hours you're back in your room," Chip said as he sewed up my arm. "But assuming everything's okay, we'll discontinue it about two P.M. Everything went well and we have fine pictures. We'll probably review them this afternoon and report to you later today or tomorrow."

I thanked Chip and his associates. It had really been an even more benign procedure than I had anticipated. I was back in my room at nine thirty and Joan was already there.

"All done," I said. "At least step one is over."

We both agreed that it was a relief to have that much behind us.

Chapter XI

July 7, 1975

I hadn't watched the monitor while the angiogram was being done, so I really had no idea what disease, if any, it had shown. Neither Chip nor his assistants made any comments at any time on what the study revealed, a policy I'm sure they adhere to rigidly. Besides, it's difficult to clearly see defects in the arteries when the fluoroscopic screen is several feet away. It takes close study and a complete review of the film to define abnormalities with any real accuracy.

I'd been lying in bed reading for about three hours—mystery, detective, and suspense stories were about all I could handle while I was in a state of suspense myself—when a

109

doctor I hadn't met before, a husky, curly-haired fellow of about twenty-nine, came in.

"Hi," he said. "I'm Rich Lewis. You don't remember me, but I've met you before. You spoke at my graduation from Tufts Medical in 1971. I'm a second-year resident in surgery." I introduced Joan, and Rich flopped down in a chair.

"I won't bother you for long," he said, "but I just called the surgical office and they told me you were now on the schedule. One of us residents see the pre-op surgicals every day, even though you're still on the medical service; just to make sure you understand what will happen and to answer questions as operating time approaches."

I think he could tell as he looked at my reaction—I suppose I looked as disappointed as I felt—that he had just broken news to me that I hadn't had. Expected news, true, but unwelcome.

"God," he said. "You mean you didn't know?"

"First I've heard," I said. "I just had the angio three hours ago."

Just then Roman came into the room, practically running. "Bill," he said, "I'm so sorry. This is exactly the sort of thing I wanted to avoid. As soon as we'd reviewed the angios I called the surgical office. I wanted to save you a place on the schedule. Then I headed right here, but of course someone held me up for a few minutes. I wanted to explain things to you first."

Rich Lewis got up. "Listen," he said, "I apologize. I'm really sorry. I'd never have come bursting in if I didn't think you knew. I'll get out now and come back later."

"It's not your fault," I said. "Don't feel bad." He seemed like a very nice fellow and I could tell he was crushed.

"No," said Roman, "don't worry. You were just doing your job."

"See you later," I said.

"Fine," Rich answered. "Nice meeting you both. Sorry, again." And he left.

"That's the way it happens sometimes," said Roman, "even with the best of intentions."

"Forget it," I said. "Just give me the news."

"It's bad and yet good," said Roman. "The bad is, of course, that you do have obstructions. Two of them. One in the left main coronary, which is about ninety to ninety-five percent complete; the other in the left anterior descending, which I'd guess is eighty percent blocked. You're going to need two by-passes.

"Some of the good news is that your right coronary is clean. No problem there. The rest is that your circumflex artery and the anterior descending, beyond the block, are both wide open. This is very important, you know. It means that once the by-passes are in, you should have excellent circulation. If your arteries weren't clean beyond the blocks, then the flow wouldn't be as predictably good."

"Then you've decided I need the operation?"

"No question, Bill," Roman said. "I'll show you the angios tomorrow, probably about six thirty in the evening. Joan, you can watch them too if you want. I want you both to be as convinced as I am.

"It's not just that you have two-vessel disease," Roman added. "It's the nature of it. We both know how highly critical the circulation to that left anterior descending artery is. I wouldn't feel at all easy leaving you with such an extensive block. What is rather amazing is that you've had such minimal symptoms with such marked disease."

"How were my collaterals?" I asked.

111

"Good," said Roman. "There's some overlap from the right coronary. But not as much as I'd expected."

"When am I scheduled?" I asked.

"Unfortunately," Roman said, "not till a week from Wednesday—the sixteenth. That's the first open spot on the schedule. We'd bump someone, because you do have marked disease, but it really isn't an emergency."

"I wouldn't want that," I said. "I'd feel guilty. I don't like waiting but I don't want to skip ahead."

"There's always the possiblity of a cancellation," Roman said. "They aren't awfully uncommon. Someone develops a complication or just decides to postpone things for family reasons. If there is a postponement, you'll be pushed ahead. In the meantime, however, I'd prefer that you stay in the hospital. I want to get a glucose tolerance test (a test for early diabetes) and a few other things. And, honestly, now that I know what you've got I wouldn't feel you were safe running around Boston. Certainly, if you have any symptoms that suggest you may be having angina, let us know immediately. If there's any threat of an infarct, we'd do you as an emergency.

"I'm going to have to run now," he said. "I'm sure you and Joan will want to talk things over."

"Before you leave," I said, "when I came down from the angio three hours ago Chip said I was to be on the monitor for a while. I told the nurse and she said a machine was on the way, but I haven't seen it yet."

"Let me listen to your heart," Roman said. He did. "It sounds fine," he said. "As long as you're okay and three hours have gone by, we'll skip the monitor. But I'll look into why you didn't have it. You should have been on it. And I'll stop in briefly before I leave this evening, in case you've come up with any questions."

When he'd gone I said to Joan, "Well, there it is. What we expected, but still a blow."

"I wish, since it's got to be done, you could have it right away."

"So do I," I said. "But I really wouldn't want to be shoved ahead of someone else; I'd feel guilty. Maybe there'll be a cancellation."

"If there isn't," Joan said, "it's going to be a long ten days."

I agreed. Then I rolled over and took a nap. The decision was made, there was nothing I could do now, and I relaxed. In a fashion.

A couple of weeks later, when I was ready to leave the hospital, one of the residents asked me if I planned to write a book about my experience.

"I'm not sure," I said. "I don't know if I'll have enough to say."

"Well, if you do," he said, "will it be pro or con the MGH?"

I hesitated. He noticed my hesitation and asked a different question. "Will it be honest?"

"Yes," I said, "it will be honest."

So, in the interest not only of honesty but completeness, I'm going to write and comment in this chapter about some of the screw-ups, the mistakes, that I saw made while I was at the General. Some, at least, are the sort of errors the lay patient might not notice. And some aren't really errors, just oversights that could be remedied with a little effort. I don't write about them to be vindictive; I'm very grateful for the fine care I received as a patient. I hope what I say will be regarded as constructive criticism, although after thinking about some of these things for several weeks, I really don't see any certain solution that would enable us to make hospitals the error-free places we'd like them to be.

One of the first foul-ups occurred on the morning of my angio, July 7. I had been fasting from eight the previous evening, because I knew Roman had ordered that a blood triglyceride study be done on me in the morning. When the stretcher came to take me to the angio room, I told the nurse on duty that the lab technician hadn't yet taken my blood.

"She can get it when you get back then," Miss X (I don't recall her name) said. I said nothing, though I was skeptical that they'd be able to run a valid triglyceride test after I'd been injected with the angio dye.

When I came back from the angio, I told Miss X that now, perhaps, they could draw the triglyceride so that I could have my breakfast. Chip had told me that the stress of the angio would probably cause a false elevation of my triglyceride, but since I'd now been fasting for fourteen hours I decided I'l like to have it done and over with if possible. Miss X went to call the lab technician and I lay back on my bed to wait.

About ten minutes later my breakfast was brought in, even though the technician still hadn't drawn the blood. I asked the aide who brought the breakfast to check with Miss X and see if I should eat. The answer came back, "Yes, it's okay to eat." Still, I waited five minutes and then buzzed Miss X myself. "Are you sure it's okay for me to eat?" I asked. "They still haven't drawn my blood."

"They haven't?" she said. "Well, your lab slip has been taken down" (off the wall to which they're apparently tacked in the morning). "Let me go check."

A few minutes later she returned.

114

"There's another doctor in the room next to you. Apparently the lab tech thought he was you. I asked your neighbor and he said that someone had drawn blood from him a few minutes ago, though he hadn't expected it and didn't know what it was for. They'll be right back to draw yours. It's all straightened out now."

Sure, it was straightened out, but only because I knew enough to know something was getting mixed up. Otherwise my neighbor's blood would have gone to the lab with my name on it and I would have gotten credit for his triglyceride level.

Important? It might have been very important as far as my future management went. If my neighbor had a low triglyceride and mine was high, my doctor might never have known what one of my troubles is. (As it turns out, elevated triglyceride levels are a problem of mine, though I'm sure Roman would have discovered that despite one lab error. A less competent cardiologist might not.)

When slipups occur, it's often impossible to determine which individual was ultimately responsible for the error. Usually so many people are involved in even the simplest procedure—each with his or her own memory of how things were done—that irrefutably pinning blame on one person is impossible.

For example, I still don't know whose fault it was that the triglyceride determination wasn't done in November when I had had my complete physical examination. Perhaps my doctor had forgotten to order it; maybe the technicians failed to draw the proper blood sample; conceivably someone in the laboratory might have dropped the test tube on the floor. It's even possible—as had almost happened here—that the test was done on my blood and recorded in the record of another patient. Unraveling these mysterious errors would baffle even Nero Wolfe.

The best that can be done is to let everyone who was involved know that a potentially serious error has been committed; in all probability the guilty party will know who he or she is and, it is to be hoped, will try to do better in the future.

Medications were a recurring problem. Roman would tell me in the morning if he had decided to add new medication, or discontinue or cut down on my old. Later, when my pills were delivered, on several occasions I'd find that his orders hadn't been carried out. I recognized most of the pills and those I didn't recognize I'd ask about. Then the nurse would go and check again. Sometimes someone, perhaps a surgical resident, had written an additional order of which I was unaware. Usually, however, I was correct and the nurse had missed or misinterpreted the order. This happened at least five times in the week I was in Phillips House.

Let me emphasize that the medications that were mis-delivered were neither essential nor potentially dangerous. Twice the nurse brought me a blood-pressure-lowering medication that Roman had told me he discontinued; twice a pill that was supposed to help me lose fluid was brought to me after it had been discontinued; once or twice tranquilizers and/or sleeping pills were not given to me even though they had been promised. If these errors had not been discovered for a long period of time, they might have proven dangerous, but since medication orders are reviewed on a daily basis at the General (a practice that is not but should be routine in every hospital), a long period without discovery was impossible. Medications of which a single dose can be critical—e.g., heart stimulants and/or anticoagulant pills—were never misdelivered.

I never checked to find out who was responsible for the errors. I simply reported them.

I suspect that sometimes the doctor failed to order or cancel a medication as he had promised; I know that I've been responsible for this sort of oversight many times.

What happens is that as I make rounds in the morning one patient may tell me she hasn't been sleeping well, so I promise her a sleeping pill; another needs a laxative; a third wants to get back on her tranquilizers. Unless I have their charts with me, and write the orders as I'm talking to them, I sometimes forget by the time I get back to the nurse's station, where I sit and write orders and progress notes, that I've promised sleeping pills, laxatives, or tranquilizers to these patients. The next day the patient tells me that she didn't get her medicine, and this time I write the order— usually.

The nurses who have to record the medication orders and give the pills to the patients will sometimes note omissions and phone the doctor to ask about the order. For example, if I have a patient who is scheduled for an operation the next morning and I've forgotten to write any preoperative orders for enemas, sedation, etc., the nurse on the evening shift will invariably call and remind me to do so. This has happened hundreds of times since I've been in practice.

But the fact that these relatively unimportant errors occur proves that the potential for serious error certainly exists; and most doctors know of at least one or two cases where such errors have happened.

Since I knew the potential for mistreatment with pills existed, I checked my pills each time and found, as I said, some errors. There's no reason why every patient shouldn't do the same. Just ask his or her doctor what medication they should be getting and how often, and if too many or not enough pills show up at any time, demand an explanation. The patient can—and I believe should—act as one more link in the chain of security in the hospital. To repeat, all humans are fallible—doctors and nurses included—and the more safeguards there are, the better.

One of the most serious cases of medication misadventure I've had in my practice involved the eighty-year-old mother of a physician. I had operated on and removed a cancer of the colon from this woman, whom I'll call Hilda. In the postoperative period she was nervous and anxious and so was her son, one of my associates. I ordered a tranquilizer to be given to her every four hours but after the order I had written "p.r.n." I don't know exactly what p.r.n. stands for but in medical practice it means, "Give only as necessary." Routinely, for example, I write "p.r.n." after a sleeping-pill order; then the pill is given only if the nurse and the patient agree it's necessary.

Unfortunately, the nurse who recorded my order onto the medication list did not include the "p.r.n." Two days later Hilda was so groggy that she could neither speak nor think clearly; she couldn't even get out of bed. Her son and I both thought that she had had a stroke—till I reviewed the orders and found that she had been receiving the tranquilizer every four hours around the clock, i.e., six times a day, much too great a dose for a woman of eighty.

The nurse responsible for the error was apologetic, but when I reviewed my written order I had to concede that the "p.r.n.," though written, wasn't as legible as it might have been. Another example of how human fallibility—to which

I don't believe there is any answer—can lead to serious errors.

There is one point I want to make with particular emphasis and this is probably an appropriate time to make it.

Before I became a patient, I sincerely felt that the doctors and nurses who took care of patients were so concerned about the patient's welfare that there was no reason for the patient to worry too much about himself; that once in the hospital, in the care of medical professionals, the patient could put his mind at ease and let someone else do the worrying. (I am making this typical patient a male because I hate to keep writing "him or herself," and I am a male.)

This is simply not true. Doctors and nurses worry about the patients under their care. They are professionals and it's their job to do what can be done to make patients well. (This reminds me of a *New Yorker* cartoon I once saw in which, as I remember it, a husband was shown shouting at his wife, "Of course, I love you, damn it. I'm your husband; it's my job to love you.") But, concerned as they are, they aren't nearly as concerned about the health of the patient as is the patient himself. I can say this with some authority since I have taken care of thousands of patients in my professional career, and though I think I am at least as compassionate and concerned about my patients as the average physician, I know I never worried about one of them as intensely as I, as a patient, worried about myself.

The doctors and nurses at Massachusetts General Hospital; Bill Petersen, my internist in Minneapolis; my partners in the Litchfield Clinic; everyone who has at any time guarded my health and well-being—all, I'm sure, have been concerned about me and have done their very best to make me well. But all their concern, added together, if it were compared to my concern about myself, would be like a drop of water compared to an ocean.

That is why, when you're a patient, you ought to count the pills, ask the reason when x-rays are ordered, and demand thorough explanations of what will be done in the course of your operation. There is no one in the entire world as concerned about your health and welfare as you are. That's the way the world is. We all look out best for number one.

I cannot resist telling finally of one patient I had who was the victim of a medication mixup. This patient, a thirty-two-year-old man, had come to me late one evening suffering from a perforated ulcer that had already produced generalized peritonitis. I operated on him that night and closed the hole in his stomach, but I had to reoperate on him twice over the next few weeks to drain abscesses that formed in his abdominal cavity. When he was finally ready to go home he was still very weak and, as is often the case when patients have been in the hospital for a long time and napping part of each day, he had difficulty sleeping at night. When I discharged him I gave him two prescriptions: one for a vitamin capsule, another for a sleeping pill.

Two weeks later when he came to my office for a checkup, I asked how he was doing. "I'm a little stronger," he said, "but I still have a terrible time getting to sleep at night. Then, half an hour after I get up in the morning I'm so tired that I can hardly keep my eyes open and I have to lie down and take a nap."

"Maybe I'd better give you a sleeping pill for a while," I said. I'd forgotten what medicines I had given him.

"You already did, Doc," he said. "In fact, I brought them with me." He handed me the two containers.

I looked at the labels and then opened the containers. On the container that contained the sleeping pills was the vitamin pill label, "Take one each morning"; and on the bottle containing the vitamin tablets was the label, "Take one each night as necessary for sleep." It was no wonder he needed a nap a half-hour after he'd gotten up.

I called the pharmacist—it was not a local drugstore—and told him what he'd done. He was very apologetic; he had been on vacation at the time and a substitute had put the pills in the wrong bottles. I put new labels on the bottles and my patient was able to give up his early morning naps.

Next, the episode with the monitor, I knew it was routine in most hospitals to put a patient who has just had an angiogram on a constant monitoring EKG. After all, an angio is an invasion of the heart. Even if not apparent immediately, damage can be done. It's only a reasonable precaution to watch the heart closely after such a test.

Nurse X at the Phillips House didn't follow up on the monitor as she should have. Preferably, it would have been waiting for me when I got back to the room, but certainly when it wasn't delivered within ten minutes of my return, she should have been on the phone tracking it down; she should have sent someone after it if she couldn't go herself. I knew I should have been on a monitor and I should have raised more hell myself. But I felt well, knew my heart rhythm was okay, and so wasn't overly concerned.

I told Roman about the triglyceride mixup and the monitor, not because I like being a squealer but because I thought he should know; and he raised the devil in the appropriate places.

Now, an important point. All these screw-ups occurred while I was in the Phillips House. Patients in the Phillips

House are often sick, but usually not acutely ill, so that critical emergencies are rare. All the rooms are private, and at $154 a room most of the people in them have to be reasonably well off. While you're a patient in the Phillips House you're kept comfortable, but you're not getting the closest, tightest, most conscientious care available at the General.

Nurses and aides who are looking for a soft spot to work, people who don't want daily crises to deal with, tend to gravitate to the parts of a hospital where such tension is least likely to be found. The dermatology outpatient division would be another example of a place where the working nurse would be unlikely to encounter an emergency.

In the only other parts of the hospital where I spent any time—the OR, the recovery room, and Baker 12—I never once noticed anything that remotely made me wonder if a screw-up was occurring. (Of course, I didn't notice much of anything in the OR.) The nurses, the aides, the technicians in these high-tension places know that a single medication mixup can, literally, mean the difference between life and death for a patient. The people who work in these places are always dedicated, intelligent, and alert. A misfit occasionally slips in, but he or she doesn't last long. A careless nurse in a recovery room stands out like a boil on the end of a nose.

We are, unfortunately, never going to make medical or surgical practice error-free—not as long as humans, who ultimately have to draw the blood, do the lab tests, pass out the pills, prescribe the medicines, and do the operating, are as fallible as we presumably always will be.

The best that can be done is what is routinely done now. The nurses who aren't ranked A+ get assigned by the nursing supervisor, who must be a good judge of people, to the places like the Phillips House where they can do little or no harm. (Though even in the Phillips House the majority of the nurses and aides were conscientious, intelligent, hardworking people.) The doctors at the top of the ladder, the chiefs of the various services, have to do the same with the people under them. We can't have a hospital staffed with all A+ people at every level; there aren't enough to go around. But we can keep the less capable and responsible people out of places where they can do harm. Or at least we can try.

One point that can be made about any hospital (or business, for that matter) is that the level of quality is determined by who's on the top. If the top people are conscientious, hardworking, capable, pleasant, efficient, they're going to choose for the rank immediately beneath them people of similar quality; and that same influence is going to be felt right down the line to the people who are for a variety of reasons—perhaps because they're uneducated or immigrants with a language problem—at the bottom of the hospital social economic ladder. But if the people who are chiefs of departments are high quality, the people who sweep up in the kitchen will do their jobs as well as they can be done. One of the reasons I felt secure at the General despite these mixups was because I knew how good the people at the top had to be just to be there.

One last point: Hospitals are, of necessity, run to suit the convenience of the doctors whenever it's reasonable to do so. It has to be this way, since in the hospital it's generally true that the doctor's time is more valuable than the patient's. But sometimes, simply because no one thinks about it, the convenience of the patient is completely disregarded when it could just as well be considered.

If you'll allow me another personal example. My operation was eventually scheduled for nine in the morning. I wanted to get a decent night's sleep the night before surgery, since I knew I was in for a couple of rough days.

However, the young man who was to "prep" me didn't show up till about eleven P.M. He was a nice fellow, a student who worked part-time as an orderly, and we chatted as he shaved me. (The prep for an open-heart procedure involves a shave from ankles to neck, front, back, and sides, followed by a painting with an amber-colored antiseptic.) When he'd finished I asked if I weren't to have an enema as I'd been warned would be the case.

"No one mentioned it to me," he said.

"Maybe someone changed his mind," I replied. "The laxative worked well."

He left and a few minutes later Miss X came in to check his work. "He didn't shave your back," she said. "Did he give you an enema?"

"No," I answered. "He said it hadn't been mentioned."

"Well, we'll have to get him or someone else back."

So it was finally 12:30 A.M. before I'd had the complete prep and enema, following which the nurse came in and gave me an injection of an antibiotic, a large, painful dose in each buttock; the shots really hurt and made my buttocks ache. I asked for some pain medicine along with my sleeping pill, and by the time she found a resident to write the order it was 1 A.M.

As a patient, I protest. The orders for my prep should have been clear, so it could be done at one session. The enema could have been given three hours earlier, so I didn't have to get out of bed repeatedly for half an hour after midnight to evacuate my bowels. The antibiotic shots could as

124

easily have been given at ten so the soreness would have diminished before I was ready to try and sleep. All of these considerations could have been given me as a patient without disrupting the proper functioning of the hospital.

Perhaps just before a patient is discharged from the hospital, he or she might be given some sort of card to fill out on which they could register their suggestions and/or complaints, as is the policy now in some hotels. Assuming these cards were screened by someone in authority (admittedly, a major assumption) I have no doubt that some worthwhile suggestions would be made, suggestions that could be implemented without disrupting any necessary hospital routines. (For example, if my suggestion was followed, there would now be a policy that no preoperative enemas be given after midnight except in emergency cases.)

Patients might also be invited to compliment or criticize in writing the doctors, nurses, and aides who had worked with them. Admittedly there would be some unjust criticism because it was uninformed; this would be recognized as such by the reviewer. But it might be good for doctors, nurses, and aides to realize that they were going to be rated on the compassion and courtesy they had or hadn't shown to their patients. The longer I think about it, the more merit I think this idea has.

Physicians and nurses owe their patients simple courtesies that we often now overlook. As a physician, I've been just as guilty as my confreres. I apologize.

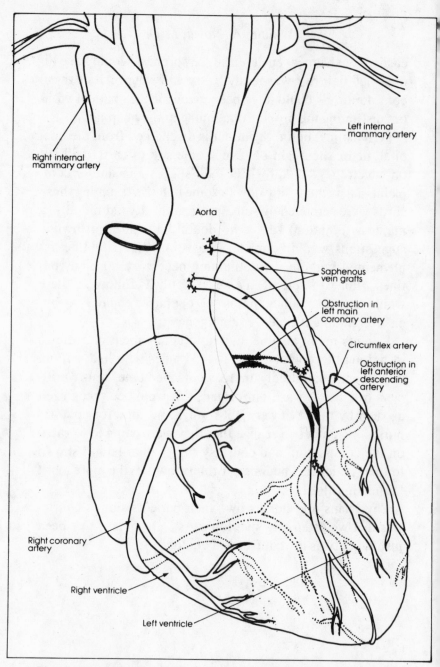

Left internal
mammary artery

Right internal
mammary artery

Aorta

Saphenous
vein grafts

Obstruction in
left main
coronary artery

Circumflex artery

Obstruction in
left anterior
descending
artery

Right coronary
artery

Right ventricle

Left ventricle

The drawing illustrates my own case of coronary artery disease and the bypasses which were done. The two new grafts bypass almost complete obstructions in the left main and anterior descending coronary arteries. The right coronary artery is free of arteriosclerotic disease.

Chapter XII

July 7, 1975 (continued) – July 8, 1975

About six thirty in the evening Rich Lewis returned to my room.

"Can't tell you how sorry I am about breaking the news to you that way," he said.

"Forget it," I said. "It wasn't your fault. I sort of expected the news anyway. There wasn't any way to break it that wouldn't have hurt."

"Just so we've got it straight," Rich said, "you know you're scheduled for a double cabbage?"

"Yes, I know. Roman told me."

(Interns and residents are great at composing slang phrases. At the General and I suppose elsewhere, a coronary-artery by-pass [CAB] done with a vein graft is known as a "cabbage"; a by-pass in which the left internal mammary artery [LIMA] is used is called a leema, as in Lima, Peru.)

He sat down in a chair. "How long have you been going?" I asked.

"Since five thirty this morning," he said. "I live a little bit out of town, half an hour's drive and rounds start promptly at six thirty A.M."

"What's your schedule?"

"Same as yours used to be," he said. "Every other night, every other weekend. You may catch four or five hours on your nights on call."

"Does it bother you?" I asked.

"No," Rich said, "I'm used to it. Everyone around here works hard, the staff men as well as the rest of us. I'm just damn glad to be here. You know, I'm the first Tufts medical graduate they're ever taken on the surgical program at the General?"

"Congratulations," I said. "I didn't even consider applying when I graduated."

"Now," Rich said, "I've got to do the surgical physical, if you know what I mean—check on those things the medical men skip over."

"I know what you mean," I said. "Like the rectal."

"Yeah," he said, "the rectal."

"I've got news for you. The medical resident did it."

"He did?" Rich said, genuinely surprised. "That's fine. Then I won't bother you. But I do want to listen to your heart and take a look at your legs. I may be the guy who will be cutting out the vein grafts."

Rich checked me over. My veins were okay.

128

"Mind answering a couple of questions?" I said.

"Not a bit," he said. "Shoot."

"All right. Tell me honestly how good an operator is El-dredth Mundth?" I'd never seen him operate and I knew Rich had watched him dozens of times. I knew, because I'd once been a resident like Rich and the rapport between us was good, that he'd give me a straight answer.

"Great," he said. "You've got no worries. He's as smooth as glass. Actually all the staff men are good, though there's one guy I don't think as much of as the others. I won't tell you his name, because he won't be anywhere near your case."

"Who will open me up?" I asked. I knew that in a teaching hospital or at any of the big clinics the surgeon of record doesn't open or close the patient, as Frank Johnson had done at Brooks. Mundth would scrub in when my chest was open, do the anastomoses (i.e. sew the grafts in place), and leave.

"Usually one of the senior residents," Rich said, "but I think in your case it will be Cary Akins, the chief resident. He's a fine operator. I'm sure he'll be in to see you.

"One other thing," Rich added. "Dr. Mundth will stay in the operating room, scrubbed in, till you're off the pump. In some places, as we both know, the surgeon drops out before the patient is off the pump."

"I wouldn't like that," I said.

"Neither would I," said Rich.

A heart operation, is in my opinion, unlike any other sort of surgery; if I didn't feel that way I'd hardly write a book about it. For example, I certainly couldn't imagine writing a book about having my gallbladder removed.

The heart is a symbolic organ. We may say as we sometimes do, "It's just a pump," and in a way we're correct. But, like the brain, we traditionally regard the heart with awe and reverence.

And, or course, I didn't like the idea of anyone operating on my heart. I accepted it as a necessity, but I didn't like it.

What I particularly disliked about the operation was the idea that at some point my heart would be stopped. It had been beating about seventy times a minute for forty-seven years, keeping me alive, and now someone was going to invade my chest and, for an hour, more or less, stop my heart. For that hour I would be dependent for continued life on the proper functioning, not of an organ made by God (or Nature, if you prefer) but on machinery put together by people, by people as fallible as we all know people to be.

And then, once the definitive portion of the operation was over, my heart would have to be restarted. It would be shocked with specially designed electric paddles and, hopefully, would resume beating again; and, again hopefully, just as efficiently as it had before the surgeons had intervened and arrested it.

If there is any single most critical moment in an open-heart operation it is that moment when the paddles are applied, the heart is shocked, and everyone—surgeons, nurses, anesthesiologists—stare down at that fist-sized organ, watching and waiting to see if it will resume its beating. There is an almost audible sigh of relief from everyone in the room when, as it usually does, the heart begins to function again as it had before the arrest.

And, just as there are sighs of relief when the shocked heart resumes its beat, so there are signs of frustration and despair when after the shock the heart resumes for a few seconds a weak, irregular beat and then reverts to its state of arrest. This is crisis time and everyone in the operating room, except the patient, knows it.

There are things to be done in these crises, and what is done and in which order will depend on the judgment and experience of the surgical team. Perhaps the by-pass pump will be restarted for a few minutes, and a second, maybe a third, attempt at shocking the heart will be made. With a high possibility of success.

If that doesn't work, the heart may be injected with stimulants, massaged by hand, poked and prodded manually, electrically, chemically. If a beat can be restarted that, though weak, is at least regular, an auxiliary supportive balloon pump may be inserted in the femoral artery, passed up the aorta, and inflated. The balloon will augment the weak heartbeat so that the chest can be closed. Hopefully, hours later the heart's beat will be back to full strength and the pump can be removed. Roman warned me before surgery that the pump had been developed at the MGH, and that it was rather freely used. He didn't want me to be shocked if I woke up and found it in place.

Finally, of course, there are those hearts that, for reasons not always fathomable, simply will not resume beating despite everything that is done to them. The heart lies there, in appearance like any other postoperative heart, but it will not beat. When that happens, when all attempts at resuscitation fail, the patient must be pronounced dead.

I was very happy to know that at General the surgeon stayed, scrubbed into the operation, until the heart was once again beating.

"Actually," Rich said, "between Dr. Mundth and Dr.

Desanctis you've got as good a team as there is in this place; I'd guess as good or better than you'd find anywhere in the world.''

With that he stood up. "Still got a lot of patients to see back in the main hospital. How do you like it over here in Phillips House?''

"Fine," I said, "but I think if I were really sick I wouldn't want to be here. I'd rather be in another section.''

"It didn't take you long to figure that out, did it?'' Rich asked. "I can tell you this. If I were dragged into this hospital half dead after an accident, I'd a lot rather be down on the ward in Bullfinch [the oldest section] with the poor people than up here with the rich.

"But don't worry," he added. "After your operation you'll go to the recovery room first, then in a day or two, depending on how fast you come along, over to Baker Twelve. You don't have to worry about the care in either place; it's the best.

"Tomorrow I'll be in the operating room all day and the other assistant resident, Greg Scott, will see you. One of us will see you every day till your operation. So, if you think of any questions, you'll have plenty of time to ask them.''

"Thanks, Rich," I said. He waved and left.

I really liked Rich Lewis, Greg Scott, Cary Akins, and all the other residents I met during my stay at the General. They all worked hard every day from 6:30 A.M. to 6:30 P.M. at least, plus every other night. But I never once heard one resident complain about the schedule. They were there to do things, to learn things, to observe, to take increasing responsibility, and they knew that the long hours were part of the game. I think they'd have felt cheated if they had been

132

cut back to ten hours a day and were only allowed to work every third night.

I know that when I had been an intern and resident at Bellevue between 1953 and 1960 I, and the other residents I had worked with, wouldn't have wanted lighter schedules. There was simply too much to learn and do in the five years allotted to our training. Sure, we complained about the work load, the menial jobs we had to do, the long hours, but we didn't want things changed.

That's why—if you'll excuse another digression—I was ashamed of and for the resident doctors who went on strike in New York in the spring of 1975. They claimed they wanted better equipment and conditions for their patients, a goal no one could disagree with but hardly one to be gained by striking. But they also wanted shorter hours, including no more than one duty night in three, for themselves. They claimed they needed the shorter hours so that they could work more efficiently on their patients' behalf.

"That," I said to myself when I read it, "is nonsense." I've never yet known a doctor to hurt a patient because he, the doctor, was working too hard. The doctor that hurts the patient is the one who won't leave his bed at three A.M. to go and see a sick patient. And I'd bet that the striking doctors, or at least those that led the strike, were of that kind. I haven't changed my mind; and I am willing to wager that no resident at Mass General, or at any of the other great teaching hospitals in the United States, will ever go out on strike.

About ten in the morning Roman called me from his office in the hospital. "Bill," he said, "we've got a break. There's been a cancellation in the operating schedule and you can be done either Thursday afternoon or Friday morning. Personally, I'd prefer to wait till Friday but it's up to you."

"No question," I said, "I'm a morning person myself, at my best before noon. Let's wait till Friday."

"Fine," Roman said. "I'll confirm it. And I'll be along this evening to show you the angio."

Anytime I'm given a choice, as a surgeon, between operating in the morning or in the afternoon, I choose the morning, when I'm most alert: Some surgeons prefer the afternoon. Perhaps Eldredth Mundth was an afternoon man, but I'd bet that most of the operating-room crew would be morning people. Besides, if they were going to do two, possibly three, open hearts that day, even though some of the team members would change, some would undoubtedly stay on, and they couldn't help but be a bit fatigued.

Finally, if I were done as the first case in the morning, I could be sure what time my operation would start; as the second patient, my starting time would have to be estimated and I'd have a long morning to get through. All things considered, Friday morning seemed great.

Now that we knew the operation was definitely scheduled for Friday morning, we called my sister Mary, who planned to come down Thursday night to stay with Joan through the operation, and then called my mother.

I really didn't want my mother to come down for the operation. I thought that worrying about me would take too much out of her. So I was prepared to argue against her making the trip.

To my surprise, when I broke the news to her she took it very calmly. In fact she said, "Do you mind if I don't come down? You know, with Jimmy's wedding coming up the next week I hate to go to a hospital and run the risk of catching a cold. I'll come down and see you when you're recuperating."

"Fine," I said, "that's very reasonable."

I hung up, told Joan what she had said, and we both laughed—not at her but at ourselves.

It's so easy when you're facing a major operation, to think that everyone is going to be as worried and concerned as you are. Far from it! It's like going on a plane flight; no one ever worries about the safety of someone who's making a flight except the passenger. A patient—like a passenger on an airplane—doesn't see things in perspective. Understandably.

We had to laugh to think that after all the time we'd spent worrying about breaking the news to my mother—afraid that she'd cry and carry on, worried about her eldest son— her big concern was not my operation but fear that she'd catch a cold before my brother's wedding. I still smile when I think of it.

Later that afternoon Dr. Mundth dropped in, introduced himself, and sat down to talk. Eldy, as he's called, is about forty-three and a little bit (at least) overweight. He's a native of Wisconsin, Harvard-educated, and trained at the General. He had not only specialized in cardiac surgery, he was for the present doing nothing but by-pass surgery. Just before I had left Minnesota I had read the first installment of a three-part article on coronary-artery by-pass surgery that he and Jerry Austen, the chief of the Department of Surgery, were publishing in the *New England Journal of Medicine*, one of the most prestigious medical journals published in the United States. I readily admit knowing that Dr. Mundth was writing this comprehensive review impressed me; I knew that to have his review published he had to know at least as much about the operation as anyone else in the country.

After we'd introduced ourselves, Dr. Mundth asked if there was anything special I wanted to ask about.

"Well, yes," I said. "In talking to other surgeons and in reading about the operation I've been impressed that so many seem to prefer to use the internal mammary artery rather than a vein. How do you feel about that?"

"We sometimes use internal mammaries," he said, "or at least some of the staff do. But I prefer, particularly in a big patient who is going to want to be quite active postoperatively, to use a vein. I think we can get more blood flow through a vein. I've been disappointed with the amount of blood that comes through some of the internal mammaries. As you know, it really isn't usually a very big artery. Admittedly, some studies have shown that the internal mammary grafts stay open in a higher percentage of cases; but our experience with veins is getting better and I suspect we're going to find, when we finish a current review of our work, that the long-term results won't be much different as far as staying open is concerned, and that the vein-graft patients, overall, will do a bit better."

"What about using the vein from the lower leg rather than the thigh? I've heard surgeons argue that because the size of the lower vein more nearly approaches that of the artery, it makes a smoother graft."

"True, initially," Eldy said, "but one of the things we know happens is that intimal hyperplasia [thickening of the inner wall of the vein] does develop with time and this, of course, narrows the caliber of the vein. So, though the initial match between the lower saphenous vein and the coronary artery may be close, we think with intimal hyperplasia to worry about we're better off using the larger portion of the saphenous from the thigh.

"Besides," he added, "it's easier to work with the larger vein."

"No more questions," I said. "Those were the things that concerned me most."

Eldy stood up. "I've got to get going," he said. "I've got another case this evening. I'll try to see you again before Friday." And he was off to the operating room.

About six thirty in the evening Roman came by. "Shall we go look at the angiogram?" he asked.

"I'm ready," I said, though I wasn't really anxious to see it. There was something about seeing a film of my own heart beating that didn't appeal to me. But I thought that perhaps if anything ever did go wrong later with the graft, I'd accept the news with more equanimity if I had seen a "before" picture.

Joan was included in his invitation, but she said, "No, thanks. I'd just as soon not look."

We walked up to the room in another wing of the hospital where angio films were kept and Roman turned on a small screen, picked my videotape film from the file, and showed it to me.

There it was, indisputable, a very clear block in the left main artery and another farther down in the anterior descending. In fact, considering the degree of the block, which was easily determined by viewing the film from several angles, it seemed amazing to me that as much dye got by as was actually the case. And it was reassuring to see the clear runoff below the blocked arteries. Roman naturally emphasized the positive findings.

As we walked back to the Phillips House together I said, "I guess there isn't any doubt I need the operation, is there?"

"No," he said, "there isn't. Sure, it's possible you could go for years, if we treated you medically and if you cut back on your activity; many people with angina lived long, reasonably active lives before this operation was ever developed. But you know as well as I that we have to deal with statistics. On the basis of everything we know now, your chances of living a long, healthy, active life are far better with the surgery than without."

"And, actually," I added, "assuming I survive the operation, even if the graft shuts down later, I'm no worse off than I would have been without the operation."

"True," said Roman, "but with your anatomy the way it is—with clean arteries beyond the block—the chances that your grafts will stay open are excellent."

This brings up another point about statistics of which I had to remind myself time and again: Statistics are just figures, and we have to be careful how we apply them.

Assume, for example, that the overall mortality rate for by-pass surgery is 10 percent; i.e., one out of 10 patients dies. Any series on which this figure was based would include a lot of patients older than I am, with more diffuse disease, many of whom had had previous infarcts. In a series composed of men of forty-seven, otherwise in good health, who had never had a coronary and had clean vessels beyond the block, the mortality would probably be well below 1 percent. So that figure, less than 1 percent, was actually closer to the true risk I was running in undergoing the operation than a figure of 10 percent.

By this time I had, as you might suspect, read all I could find about the results of coronary-artery by-pass operations. Happily, the statistics were not only encouraging but convincing.

I knew, for example, that with blocks like the ones I had, with medical treatment my chances of dying within one year were about 13 percent. With a successful operation, my chances of dying within a year would be reduced to 2 percent. Since, at forty-seven, my chances of dying within a year were 1.3 percent even if I didn't have coronary-artery disease, the operation would reduce my risk of dying within one year almost to normal.

I also knew what the five-year mortality figures were like. These were just beginning to accumulate. After all, the operation was only developed in 1967 and hadn't really been done very extensively until 1969, but so far the results were impressive. Representative figures, as I'd dug them out of the medical and surgical literature, looked like this:

	Surgical Treatment	Medical Treatment
Three-vessel disease	83%	40%
Two-vessel disease	92%	65%
Preinfarction angina; i.e., patients whose angina is rapidly getting worse	90%	70%
One-vessel disease*	92%	88%

*Even though the surgical treatment of one-vessel disease is not significantly better than medical treatment, most physicians have concluded that if the one vessel involved is the left main coronary artery, surgery should be done. Left main disease is, in effect, like having two-vessel disease, since a block here impedes flow to both the circumflex and the anterior descending coronary arteries. (See illustration on p. 126.) *Footnote continued on next page.*

With odds like these, I'd have been an idiot to refuse the operation.

It seems odd, I suppose, to continually refer to statistics when writing about health, medicines, and operations, but actually statistics are fundamental to all medical and/or surgical care.

Consider, as a simple example, the patient who comes to me with a hernia. When I advise that patient as to whether or not he should have an operation to correct his defect, I have to take into consideration his age, his general health, how much pain or discomfort the hernia is causing him, and what will likely happen to him and his hernia in the future. I weigh the contraindications for the operation—the surgical risk of morbidity and mortality in this particular patient—against the potential benefits—relief of pain and discomfort, freedom from the threat of a possible strangulation (twisting of intestine in the hernia sac); and then advise the patient as to whether or not I think he should have the operation. He has the right to accept or reject my advice.

Consider the woman who has a chest x-ray taken for some innocuous reason—say, as a routine part of an insurance examination—and I note incidentally that she has stones in her gallbladder. Some gallstones, if they happen to contain calcium, can be seen on routine films of the upper abdomen; to visualize most gallstones, it's necessary that the patient take pills containing a dye that is then concentrated in the gallbladder.

Let's assume this woman has absolutely no symptoms

Some surgeons also feel that if the one-vessel disease is in the anterior descending coronary artery, surgery should be done. The left anterior descending coronary artery is sometimes referred to as the artery of sudden death. An acute block of the artery is often quickly fatal as opposed to a block in the right or circumflex arteries, which may cause infarction but not death.

that suggest gallbladder disease. She has never had a gall-bladder "attack," never even suffered from mild indigestion. Should she now undergo an abdominal operation to have a completely asymptomatic gallbladder removed?

The decision is, of course, hers to make. But I would give her advice based on statistical evidence that has accumulated in the medical literature over the years. These statistics show that so-called silent gallstones do not usually remain silent. Most gallstones that are discovered incidentally will, in a matter of months or possibly years, cause trouble. Sometimes they produce relatively minor symptoms, sometimes major problems. So, if the woman is relatively young and healthy (and "young" is in itself a relative term that can mean anything from forty-five to sixty-five), I would probably advise her to have her gallbladder removed even though it was not troubling her. I'd base my advice on statistics which show that in all probability she will have trouble later, at which time she will be older, the gallbladder itself may then be acutely inflamed and more difficult to remove, and the risk of the operation—well under 1 percent in a healthy woman—might be in the 3 to 5 percent range. She may also, if she waits, develop complications such as jaundice, which add significantly to the risk of the operation.

She will, of course, be free to reject my advice. If she does she may, twenty or thirty years later, still have had no gallbladder trouble and she will be free to laugh at me. She will have made a bet with herself, so to speak, and will have won, even though the odds were against her. But, if ten similar patients came to me with the same problem and all ten rejected my advice, the chances are that seven or eight of the ten would live to regret their decision.

Everything we do in medicine is a matter of statistics. Whenever we prescribe a pill or an operation, we have mentally weighed the benefits to be gained against the risks inherent in either the pill or operation and have decided that the potential benefits outweigh the potential risks. That is the way all good medicine is practiced; and the theory applies as well to surgery for coronary-artery disease as it does to prescribing penicillin for a case of tonsillitis.

The next day Jerry Austen, the chief of surgery, came in to visit with me, as he did several times during my hospitalization. Jerry is the kind of man commonly described as a dynamo. He simply exudes energy. He works fourteen to fifteen hours a day, like the men who work with him (as head of the department, he chooses most of his co-workers). Jerry is from Ohio originally, and he and Roman had been classmates at Harvard Medical School.

Jerry holds the title of chairman of the Department of Surgery at the Massachusetts General Hospital, and is also the Edward D. Churchill Professor of Surgery at Harvard. He is justly proud of both titles, but particularly, I think, of the latter, since he is the first person to hold the Churchill professorship since Churchill, a renowned name in the history of surgery, retired six years ago.

After we'd talked a few minutes I mentioned my thoughts on statistics to him.

"No question about it," he said. "You have to look very carefully at statistics to put them in their proper perspective. And it doesn't do any harm to know the people who are making the reports.

"Take our statistics, for example. Our mortality rate for by-pass isn't anything to be ashamed of, but it's not the one percent or two percent that some clinics report. I'll tell you

142

why. Right across the corridor from you is a man who was turned down for surgery last week by one of the well-known clinics with a fantastically low mortality rate. This patient is miserable. He can't do anything without his angina flaring up.

"His angiogram isn't promising. If he'd respond to medical treatment we'd be delighted, but he hasn't so we're going to operate on him. We think we can help him. We know, and he knows, that he isn't a good risk. Instead of being in the one percent or lower category, as you probably are, he's probably in the twenty percent group. But we feel, and he does, too, that the risk is worth running. Operate on enough people in his category and your statistics won't be as good as someone else's, but you'll have helped a lot of people who would otherwise be miserable. We're sure enough about the work we do here at the General not to worry about our mortality rates being a bit higher than someone else's. This doesn't mean, naturally, that we're knife-happy and will operate on just anyone. There are surgeons like that. You know them as well as I."

Since I was still a little bit concerned about the choice of a vein graft over an internal mammary, I mentioned my misgivings to Jerry.

"I know the statistics you're talking about," he replied. "As a matter of fact, I spoke to Dr. X [I'll leave his name out of this] just last week, and despite the positive tone of the articles you've read by him, he's beginning to be a bit disappointed in some of his late results. You've got to remember that this field is changing so fast that the literature has difficulty keeping up with it. Remember, there's at least a six-month lapse between the time an article is written and its publication. Things can change in six months.

"One of the things Dr. X told me is that he's now seeing patients who, despite the fact that their internal mammary grafts are staying open, are having infarcts in the areas to which the grafts go. The flow through the graft just isn't sufficient to answer the demand of the heart muscle. That's why we're doing mostly vein grafts now. If our experience changes, if we learn something new, sure, we may have to change later."

(Later, in a talk I had with Cary Akins when I mentioned my misgivings about the use of a vein graft instead of the internal mammary artery, he reminded me of something I'd forgotten.

At times of stress or excitement the arteries to inessential areas not needed for a stress reaction go into spasm; i.e., they become tighter and narrower so that less blood flows through them. The coronary arteries, under condition of stress, relax and become bigger so they can bring more blood to the heart muscle.

"How do you think an internal mammary artery acts at a time of stress?" Cary asked me.

"I don't know," I said, "but it normally goes to an inessential area, so I'd guess that it would probably go into spasm and narrow down."

"I'd guess the same," Cary said. "The study hasn't yet been done—it would be awfully difficult to do—but I suspect that we'd find the transplanted internal mammary artery tightening down just when it's needed most. That doesn't mean we're right about the vein over the artery, but it's a point worth considering.")

In one of my later conversations with Jerry, we got into his philosophy of surgical training. I mentioned one university center I knew reasonably well where the philosophy was that every would-be surgeon ought to spend at least two years in a dog lab, doing research. In fact, at more than one center, you'll find chiefs of departments who believe a surgeon can learn to operate working mostly on dogs.

"I just don't subscribe to that at all," said Jerry. "As I'm sure you know, we have our pick of the best graduates for the surgical program here. In fact, one of my toughest jobs—I share the responsibility with a committee but naturally I'm the one who has to make the final decision—is to say no to some of the excellent candidates for our program.

"But our goal here is to train doctors to take care of people. We carry on research programs in every department of the hospital; and if I have a resident who wants to spend a year or two doing research, that's fine with me. Usually I encourage him to go somewhere more research oriented and then we take him back on the program later.

"My prime interest is in producing surgeons who are going to help people. They've got to know what's going on in the world of research or else they'll fall hopelessly behind clinically; but basically they're here to learn to take care of patients. At some of these places they take on more residents than they can possibly train, just to staff dog labs. They pour out papers, usually in the chief's name, and usually not worth much as far as information is concerned. I'm dead set against that sort of thing.

"I think the basic researcher and the clinician are two different breeds. We ought to each do our own jobs. What good would it do anyone if I were to run down and spend an hour a day fooling around in a laboratory? It would be a waste of my skills and time. I can do more for people work-

145

ing here on the wards, in the operating room, and teaching. Administration is a necessary evil, but of course I have to do some of that, too.

"Once in a while we get a resident who's afraid that if he doesn't spend a year or so doing research he'll never get to be a senior resident or a chief. That's nonsense. If he wants to do some research, fine; but there's no sense doing it to score Brownie points with me, because it doesn't."

"Do you really like working as long and hard as you do?" I asked.

"I love it," Jerry said. "If I didn't, I wouldn't be here. Sometimes, I know, it's tough on our families, but we try to make it up to them otherwise. I spent this weekend up in New Hampshire at a place my wife and kids are using for a while. It was fun, but two days were enough. I wanted to be back here."

In fact, all the doctors on the staff at General, as I've already mentioned, seemed perfectly content with their twelve-to-fifteen-hour days. I admired them.

But though I admired them, it wasn't the sort of life that I'd chosen or would choose if I had it to do again. I enjoy medicine, but it isn't my whole life. I like time to read things other than medical journals, to spend a lot of time with my family, to lead a broader life than these men at General whom I admire so much, lead. They've chosen medicine to the exclusion of much else; I haven't, and neither have my partners, who enjoy time away from their medical work as much as I do.

Do Eldy, Jerry, and Roman have the right philosophy or do doctors, like those of us in the Litchfield Clinic, have the right idea? I don't think there's any right or wrong to it. I think there's room in medicine for people of both persuasions. (Let me make it clear that all the fifteen-hour workers aren't in the big city hospitals; I know many in small towns.)

Now, as a patient, with the problem I had, I was happy to be in the care of doctors with the hard-work philosophy that prevailed at the General.

Chapter XIII

July 9, 1975–July 11, 1975

Over the next two days I was kept reasonably well occupied with blood tests, lung-function tests, and regular visits from one or another of the surgeons.

I told my brother that I couldn't be best man at his wedding. He understood perfectly why I wanted to get the operation over rather than have to live with the dread of it till after his wedding on the nineteeth. He invited my son Jimmy, his godson, to substitute for me, and Jimmy agreed immediately. Jimmy is very mobile; he has gone off to California or down to Florida on a day's notice, carrying, usually, a paper bag with a few clothes in it. He gave up his job as a sod layer when he agreed to come to the wedding in Massachusetts, figuring he'd find work in Massachusetts for a while after the wedding, and he did. Sometime, I think, he'll get into the restaurant business; he's a natural as a cook and worked nights as a chef at our golf club during his last two years of high school. He's not a student, never has been, and has no desire to go to college. For now, he just wants to move around and see the country. He's twenty-one and has no entangling alliances, so I suppose there's no good reason why he shouldn't do as he wishes; not that I should control him even if I could.

My lung tests were essentially normal. I've never smoked cigarettes, and though I used to smoke cigars occasionally, I never learned to inhale them. After my lung-function tests the technician said, "Never smoked, have you?"

"Not cigarettes, no."

"Makes a big difference," he said.

I'm certain that at least twenty times during my convalescence someone said, "One of the reasons you're doing so well is that you've never smoked." Having operated on heavy smokers, many with chronic bronchitis and/or emphysema, I knew what they meant. A long history of heavy smoking frequently means postoperative lung problems.

I spent most of the ninth and tenth just sitting around my room reading or talking with Joan. I received a lot of phone calls, cards, and telegrams from Minnesota, but, of course, no visitors. I really didn't feel like having visitors, so I hadn't let anyone in Massachusetts except my immediate family know I was in the hospital. Besides, I'd been out of Massachusetts for over twenty years, and with a very few exceptions had lost all contact with friends back there.

I accepted the idea of my approaching operation quite

calmly. I was concerned, or course—there were obvious reasons for concern—but I don't think it would be true to say I was frightened. I wasn't. I knew that I would have the best of available care, and I felt that the operation was a necessary one. There was nothing more I could do so I tried, with reasonable success, not to dwell on what I'd have to go through.

The matter of explaining risks to the patient is a touchy one. Theoretically, in my case Roman or Dr. Mundth or some other responsible party should have sat down and told me all the things that can go wrong when a heart operation is done, begining with the discomfort I'd experience and ending with the possibility of death. But they assumed correctly that I knew all this.

My own policy is to tell the patient that there are certain risks associated with whatever operation I may be planning to do, and to spell out in as much detail as I think is reasonable what those risks are. But I don't dwell on the risks. I don't want to take a terrified patient into the operating room. And I always emphasize to the patient that the risk of having the operation is minimal in comparison to the risk of not having the operation. In cases where the operation is purely elective—for example, a varicose vein operation done solely for cosmetic purposes—I make certain that the patient knows that the decision is hers to make, but if the veins are unsightly and very disturbing to her emotionally, I let her know that I agree with her decision.

With the recent explosion of malpractice suits it has become increasingly difficult for a surgeon to be certain that he is not leaving himself open to a suit without frightening a patient who—just because he or she is a patient—is naturally apprehensive.

151

For example, assume a forty-year-old woman is referred to me because she has gallstones that are causing a great deal of distress. Almost every time she eats she has pain in her abdomen, and at times suffers from vomiting and episodes of pain. Her gallstones are making her miserable.

I examine her, find that aside from the gallstones she is in excellent physical condition, and recommend removal of the gallbladder.

Now, theoretically, to be sure she is giving me "informed consent" to perform the operation, I should sit down with her and go over all the complications. I ought to tell her (1) that she might die suddenly from the anesthesia; (2) that I might cut the artery to the liver, in which case her liver would die and so would she; (3) that I might leave a sponge in her abdomen, necessitating at least a second operation and a long convalescence; (4) that I might fail to tie off a blood vessel and that she would then hemorrhage postoperatively; (5) that just from lying in bed for a couple of days she might develop phlebitis, throw a blood clot to her lung, and possibly die.

These and dozens of other complications can occur during and after gallbladder surgery. Most are complications I've never seen, but they've been reported in the surgical literature so they are admittedly possibilities. But if I spelled them out to the patient, she would in all probability decide against an operation that she really ought to have. So, like most surgeons, I tell her there are risks (one technique used very commonly by surgeons is to add, "Just as there are risks in crossing a street"), but I don't dwell on them. Whether that's good enough to protect me in court when or if (heaven forbid) any of my patients ever have one of these bizarre complications, will have to be decided at that time.

With patients who are obviously critically ill but who need an operation if they are to have any reasonable chance of surviving—e.g., a seventy-year-old man with peritonitis from a perforated cancer of the stomach—most surgeons assume a very encouraging attitude with the patient, assuring him of the necessity for the operation and emphasizing, indirectly, the benefits to be gained. In this situation, for example, I'd probably talk most with the patient about how well he'll be able to eat after the operation without spending much time on the risks involved. With very sick patients, it's generally safe to assume they know they are in a precarious situation, and there's little reason to dwell on it.

With the family of the patient—and it's important whenever possible to talk with a responsible member of the family before performing any surgery—complete candor is in order. The risks should be emphasized and spelled out in reasonable detail and the potential benefits should be estimated conservatively, or even underestimated. This policy, known in medical circles as hanging a little crepe, serves two purposes. It warns the family so that they can prepare themselves for the worst and—this is admittedly selfish—it gets the doctor off the hook (if you'll excuse the phrase) if something goes wrong.

Some doctors are notorious crepe-hangers. Even if the operation is generally associated with a minimum mortality and even if the patient is an exceptionally good risk, these doctors present the case to the family as if it were the greatest challenge since Christ undertook to raise Lazarus from the dead. Then, if the patient does well—as in all probability he or she will—to the family the doctor is the greatest hero since Lindbergh. And, if the patient doesn't do well, the family simply says, "Well, Doctor, we know you did the best you could. If you couldn't save him, no one could."

In every medical community there are local heroes with greatly overinflated reputations among the general public. These people may or may not be superior doctors, but of one thing you can be certain: they are masters of the art of crepe-hanging.

When I later returned to Litchfield, I was asked by a friend who used to be a practicing Catholic if the approaching operation had made me more religious. I had to answer that it had not.

I thought, of course, about the possibility of death. I was brought up as a Catholic but I haven't practiced the formalities of my religion much in recent years. Basically, I suppose, I'm what most of the people I know (despite their formal church affiliations) seem to be: an agnostic who leans toward a belief in the afterlife. I knew there was a possibility I might die during this operation. I has no well-defined idea of what would happen to me (except in a physical sense) if that should occur. I rather believe that in one form or another my soul (and I refuse to try and define that) would continue to exist. I have, I think I can now say with more certainty than I could before the operation, lost the fear of hell and eternal suffering that was so prominent in the Catholic religion I knew as a child. I guess that entire concept, except as embodied in a few radical schismatic branches, has diminished in importance in the Catholic Church as it now exists. I know that my children go to mass rather casually and almost invariably go to communion

154

when they do attend. They seem to be at peace with their religion, and I'm delighted. When I compare their attitude with memories of my youth, the contrast is remarkable.

I remember, as a child, telling my mother that a friend of mine, John Riley, was going to the movies on Good Friday afternoon. "He'll be lucky if he doesn't turn to stone," she said. I, of course, went with all my other Catholic friends to the Good Friday afternoon session of the Stations of the Cross. I'd have been scared to go to the movies with John Riley.

My mother has mellowed a lot since then. She knows the religious habits of my children and she doesn't condemn them. On the other hand, my mother still attends mass several times a week. Her faith in her basic religion hasn't changed much.

After all that, if anyone pushed me to the wall, I'd have to say that I envy my mother. I wish I had her faith, as, I'm sure, my children wish they had it. But times change and sometimes you can't hold onto the things you'd like to.

On Thursday afternoon John Bland, who was to be chief anesthesiologist on my case, stopped in to say hello. John is English and had training both in the United States and Great Britain. He preferred to practice in the United States, and because he is very talented, was eagerly welcomed back on the staff at the General.

"You've seen enough operations, certainly, so that I won't bore you with details," he said after we'd met. "The only thing you may find unusual is that I routinely put a catheter into the lung so that we can keep a closer eye on your fluid situation than might otherwise be possible. I pass it through the skin of the neck and down into the lung through the jugular vein; it enables us to measure fluid pressure in the lung. I usually insert it just before you're put to sleep. It might give you a bit of discomfort but I promise you it won't be bad."

"I leave that up to you," I said. "I'm very much in favor of anything you want to do to make this procedure go well."

Then we got to talking about medicine in England. "How in the world, I asked him, are the English going to pay the extra medical expenses that will be generated when by-pass surgery, if it's generally accepted as I expect it will soon be, catches on?

"Here in the United States about one and a half million people have heart attacks, either infarcts or first attacks of angina, every year. Half of them die, but seven hundred thousand live. If we assume that even one-fourth of the survivors, one hundred and fifty thousand or so, would benefit from a by-pass, and if each operation cost, as it does, about ten thousand, our economy isn't going to be able to pay for it. And we're better off economically than England."

"The British simply won't be able to afford by-passes on a large scale," John said. "They've been content, so far, to let the pioneer work be done in the United States. What they'll have to do, of course, is draw more rigid lines than you do here and keep the surgery more exclusive. For example, here we'd be highly unlikely to operate on anyone over eighty. That eliminates, for medical reasons, a certain segment of the population. The British government might choose to draw the line at sixty, which would eliminate thousands of those who, in all probability, would otherwise be candidates for the operation. Or they may choose to rule out those with disease of only one vessel, which again would cut down on the number of cases they will have to pay for.

"Another approach is to limit the number of places where angiography is done. If you can't get on the schedule for an angiogram, you can hardly expect to be a candidate for by-pass surgery. To a large extent that's the situation in this country now. The number of places where angiography is done are limited, as are the facilities for by-pass surgery. The procedure still isn't widely accepted by physicians in all the small and medium-sized cities, or in many sections of the larger cities. As long as that remains the case, we won't be overwhelmed. If things change, more money will have to be spent. But the British will simply have to set limits that are more exclusive than those in the United States."

"The economics of all of medicine is going to be a problem soon," I said. "It already is, of course, but I think it will become more apparent in the near future."

"No question," said John. "I'm glad it is not, at least for the moment, my particular problem. Though, of course, it involves all of us.

"Well," he said, standing, "I shall see you tomorrow. And rest easy; I'm sure everything will go fine."

"Thanks," I said. "I expect so, too."

No one had to hang any crepe for me. I knew what would happen to me once I was asleep; I had not only read about the by-pass operation, but several months earlier—before I knew I'd ever be a candidate for the procedure—I'd watched a friend of mind do one.

First, someone—probably Cary Akins—would take a scalpel and make an incision along the length of my sternum (breastbone). This incision would go down to the

157

bone. Any bleeding vessels would be clamped and either tied or cauterized, i.e., coagulated with an electric current.

Next, Cary would take an electric saw and split my sternum along its entire length. He would then insert a metal "spreader" between the two halves and crank it open. This would expose the pericardium, a thin sac in which the heart lies. A few snips of the scissors and the sac would be opened and the beating heart exposed.

While Cary was opening my chest, another surgeon, probably a senior resident, would be operating on my thigh, removing the superficial saphenous vein. There are two sets of veins in the leg, a superficial set that lies just beneath the skin—the set that enlarges in the patient with varicose veins—and a deep set, down within the muscles. We can get along quite nicely without our superficial leg veins. The incision through which the vein is removed would run on the inside of the thigh from the groin to the knee.

Cary, or possibly Dr. Mundth, would then take the vein and cut two five- or six-inch pieces from it. Using a special clamp that blocks off only a small part of the aorta, he would then sew one end of each of the pieces of vein to the side of the aorta at two different places.

Next the surgeon would insert one end of a plastic tube into the right atrium, the chamber of the heart to which blood from the rest of the body flows. This blood would then by-pass the heart, flow through the heart-lung machine, and be pumped back to the body through a second plastic tube, one end of which would be inserted into the aorta. With the heart by-passed, it would quickly stop beating.

While the heart was arrested, Dr. Mundth would then sew the other ends of the veins he had previously attached

158

to the aorta to the sides of my left anterior descending coronary artery and my circumflex artery, beyond the points of obstruction, completing the by-pass.

With the vein grafts in place, the by-pass tubes would be clamped and, using two metal paddles, the heart would be shocked. Hopefully, it would then resume beating.

Finally, Dr. Mundth, using a special instrument, would measure the flow through the by-passes. Assuming flow was adequate, he would remove the by-pass catheters, closing the holes in the aorta and atrium as he did so. Dr. Mundth would then, in all probability, drop out of the case and Cary Akins would close my chest, using wire sutures to pull the two halves of my sternum together.

The entire operation would probably take three or four hours, but a lot of this time would be spent opening and closing the incision. I would, hopefully, only be on the pump, with my heart arrested, for about an hour. (Actually, as it turned out, I was only on the pump for forty-eight minutes.)

While I was anesthetized Dr. Bland and his co-workers would be watching my vital signs—pulse, blood pressure, and respiration rate—very carefully. They would also run regular, frequent checks of my blood to make certain that all the constituents, chiefly electrolytes and gases, stayed within normal limits.

I knew that the operation I was soon to have was a major undertaking. I knew there were risks involved and that, if things didn't go well, I might die. But I also knew that I was in an excellent hospital, under the care of dedicated, capable physicians. I was concerned, of course, but I wasn't really frightened.

My sister Mary, who is two years younger than I, arrived

159

later, shortly after Dr. Bland had left. Mary and I have always been quite close. In high school she dated my friends and I dated hers. She played piano and I played saxophone in our high school dance band. She has been out to visit us in Minnesota and we've been back to visit Mary and her husband Jack in Simsbury, Connecticut. She and Joan are good friends and Joan wanted Mary to stay with her through the ordeal of the operation.

We had a pleasant Thursday afternoon visit and they left about 9 P.M. Joan had decided, though I told her it wasn't necessary, to stop in the next morning before they wheeled me upstairs to the operating room. On Fridays the surgical staff holds its regular weekly conference, so the first operation isn't scheduled till 9 A.M. Usually, it's at 8 A.M.

I've already described my preoperative evening, enema and all, so I'll only add now that when I finally got to sleep, about 1 A.M., I slept soundly till the nurse woke me at 7:30 so that I could wash and brush my teeth before the orderly came to pick me up.

By the time Joan and Mary arrived at eight I had finished washing up and was lying in bed, waiting to be picked up. I was still quite calm. They had been there only a few minutes when the nurse arrived and gave me my preoperative medication—two more shots of an antibiotic (antibiotics are used prophylactically in open-heart cases in the hope of preventing infections); a sedative; and an injection of scopolamine, a drug with which most women who have experienced childbirth (not natural childbirth, of course) are acquainted. It very quickly dries up all one's secretions, which is the reason it's used; copious secretions in the mouth, pharynx, and lungs may interfere with the anesthesia. The scopolamine made me dry almost immediately.

160

It was a very annoying feeling and it persisted till I was put to sleep. Of all the injections I had while in the hospital, I disliked that one the most.

Almost immediately after I'd been given the shots the orderly arrived with his stretcher. Joan and I kissed goodbye, and I believe I even kissed Mary, though we are not a kissing family. Then I was trundled off to the elevator. I was drowsy but still reasonably alert. I remember the ride to the operating floor quite well.

I was not wheeled into the operating room immediately. Instead, in a sort of alcove off the OR (as I remember it) two anesthesia residents (whom I remember only vaguely, though they did introduce themselves) went to work on me, plugging in the lines, as they say in anesthesia. One put an intravenous tube in a vein in my right arm, the other worked on my left wrist or elbow putting a catheter in the artery. I am, admittedly, a bit vague on this, since the sedation was beginning to hit me.

I was then wheeled into the operating room where I was greeted by Dr. Bland. I remember others, presumably the resident surgeons and nurses standing around, but only vaguely.

Dr. Bland said, "This will hurt just a bit," and he stuck a needle through the skin of the right side of my neck as he had warned me he would. The pain of that injection, which I would describe as more of an annoyance than anythng else, was the last thing I remember till I woke up, four hours later, in the recovery room. Dr. Bland asked me, days later, if I remembered anything of the surgery. He said that at one point in the procedure my depth of anesthesia was not very great. I told him I remembered absolutely nothing.

CHAPTER XIV

July 11, 1975 (continued)–July 12, 1975

When I opened my eyes in the recovery room, it was almost exactly 1 P.M. I knew this, because the first thing I
saw was a clock on the wall facing my bed. Roman was
standing over me shouting, "It's all over, Bill. Everything
went very well." I had a tube in my throat, the tube that
had been passed through my mouth into my trachea and
through which my gas anesthetic had been given. Since the
tube went through the space between the vocal cords, push-
ing them aside against the inner wall of the trachea (windpipe), naturally I couldn't talk. I nodded to Roman, letting
him know I understood him. Then I looked around and saw
Joan and Mary standing near the bed. Roman had brought

163

them to the recovery room as soon as I reached there so that they could see that I was alive and well.

Joan looked to me as if she were scared to death and ready to cry; so did Mary. They both assured me later that is exactly how they felt. (One thing that we doctors fail to realize is that patients or incisions that look well and healthy to us, don't look very well or healthy to the lay person. We are so used to seeing very critically ill patients, patients who are literally almost dead, that we forget this is an experience lay people don't often have. So, when they see a patient with a big tube sticking out of his mouth, with smaller tubes running in or out of orifices, arteries, and veins, that patient looks to them like a very sick individual. Joan and Mary hadn't ever seen a really critical postoperative patient, so they could only compare my appearance with that of someone who was well. Naturally, by those standards I looked to them about as badly off as anyone could be.)

Joan told me she loved me a couple of times; this really wasn't the time for any involved conversations, particularly when, as she understood, I couldn't answer her. After about two minutes they left, and the nurse who was in charge of me took over. I vaguely remember the nurses who watched me through that night; I'm sure I wouldn't recognize them if I passed them on the street, but I want to pay tribute to them. They did a marvelous job.

The hours immediately after an open-heart operation are, as you'd expect, critical ones. During the procedure, particularly while the patient is on the pump, dozens of electrolytes (e.g., the sodium, chloride, and particularly the potassium in one's body) shift about in and out of the cells and bloodstream very rapidly. As this happens, water also moves in and out of the tissues. Pressures in the heart and lungs must be constantly monitored, as must the electrolyte levels. Otherwise there is a real risk that strange disruptions of heart rhythm may occur or that the patient may drown in his own fluids, (i.e. if excess fluid overloads the lungs). It is not unusual for a patient to gain ten or fifteen pounds, mostly fluid, during an open-heart operation.

These nurses were used to their jobs but that didn't make their jobs any less demanding. I had a catheter in my bladder, inserted, I assume, once I'd been put to sleep in the operating room, and they measured urine output from the bladder, and fluid intake through my various intravenous and intra-arterial lines at least every hour. Sometimes on their own, sometimes on orders from the surgical residents who moved from bed to bed checking patients, they adjusted flow rates and added new solutions, particularly those containing potassium, an electrolyte that is critical to proper heart function and moves around rather wildly after an open-heart procedure.

Another of their major jobs was to keep my lungs clear and make certain I got all the air and oxygen I needed. After most abdominal operations we routinely remove the endotracheal tube as soon as the patient is reasonably awake. We expect that he or she will have a clear airway and will breathe without difficulty.

This isn't the case after open-heart operations. It's crucial that the patient get plenty of oxygen into his bloodstream so that the heart will get the oxygen it needs, and it's not safe to trust the patient to breathe regularly and deeply on his own.

First, as I can testify, it hurts too damn much. After all, the sternum has just been split down its middle and then the two halves have been cranked apart for a couple of hours. At the end of the operation the two halves of the sternum are pulled together again and held together with strong sutures; at the General they use wire. So every time you take a deep breath or—heaven help you!—cough, you feel as if you're going to split in half. The feeling is not one you're likely to encourage by coughing or even breathing deeply if left alone.

So the tube is left in the windpipe. The nurse can and does attach it most of the time to a respirator, so that your lungs fill and empty without any effort on your part. When the respirator was on, I didn't mind the endotracheal tube too much.

But, every now and then, just to encourage me to get going on my own, the nurse would turn off the respirator and I would have to move air in and out of my lungs—breath, as it's commonly called, on my own power. I'd been breathing regularly on my own for forty-seven years, and I've even been known to pant and cough occasionally, but this was like something I'd never done before. To say it wasn't any fun would be a gross understatement. But I did it. One breathes when one is out of breath or one doesn't go on living, so I breathed. After progressively longer intervals on my own, I'd be hooked back up to the respirator.

In all my waking moments—and I was, I think, awake most of the time—I couldn't keep my eyes off the clock on the wall opposite me. Sometimes I'd shut my eyes for what I thought must be an hour and I'd open, look, and find that only ten minutes had gone by. I found it difficult to believe this clock was actually working.

The worst moments, without any doubt, were those times when my lungs would have to be suctioned. I suppose this happened every hour or two, depending on how my blood gases were—the oxygen and carbon dioxide content of the blood were regularly measured—and how high my temperature reached. Low oxygen saturation of the blood and/or an elevation in temperature usually meant that secretions were collecting in my lungs, below the endotracheal tube, and these had to be removed so that I wouldn't get pneumonia. Since I couldn't voluntarily cough with the endotracheal tube in me, the nurse would suction out these secretions by passing a rubber catheter through the endotracheal tube, down into the bronchi (the smaller branches of the trachea that extend out into the lungs). The rubber catheter was used as a suction device, like a vacuum cleaner, and when it hit the inner lining of my bronchi, it would also trigger, reflexively, a cough. This procedure hurt like hell; but it would effectively clean out my lungs and shortly thereafter my temperature would drop from 103 or so down to 99 or 100.

The nurses were not without pity. They were, as I've said, very nice. So at intervals they would give me small injections of morphine. Not enough to be put to sleep or slow down my breathing—after all, the reason for spending time in the recovery room is to gradually wake up and breathe efficiently on one's own—but enough to at least deaden the pain and, I suppose, allow me to doze off occasionally.

I'd like to say that I was comforted through all these hours by the thought that at least I had survived the operation and was doing well but to be perfectly honest I didn't think much about it. I suppose that thought occurred to me once in a while, but I certainly don't remember dwelling on it.

About 5 P.M. Joan and Mary were brought back to see how much better I was looking. They told me later that they dreaded the revisit, but Mary, who was driving back home that evening, felt obligated to stay for one more look; she had wondered if I had any chance at all after her first visit.

The second visit was a rerun of the first, though, as I failed to mention, during the first visit I had shivered a lot (the body temperature is lowered several degrees during an open-heart procedure), and by now at least I was done with that. Again Joan said, "I love you," again I nodded in what I hoped she'd interpret as an echo, and then they were gone. Those visits served a purpose, I suppose, but they weren't really very satisfactory. I was more concerned with myself than anything else; Joan's peace of mind, I'm sorry to say, was not something I was worried much about.

About 8 P.M., the nurse began to discuss with the assistant surgical resident the possibility of removing my endotracheal tube. Sometimes, if the patient is doing well, the tube is removed eight or nine hours after surgery; otherwise it is left in for twenty-four hours or, occasionally, longer.

By eight this tube had become my major nemesis. I was breathing through it on my own, without the aid of the respirator, for longer and longer periods of time, and I really felt as if I'd be able to breathe better on my own if it were removed. Besides, it hurt. In fact, the pressure of the tube on my mouth and trachea or vocal cords (I'm not sure exactly where the pain came from) was the pain that bothered me most. My chest incision and the incision in my thigh through which the vein had been removed hurt, naturally, but not as much now as did the tube.

About 9 P.M. they tested my ability to breathe on my own by having me exhale through the tube into a machine. They tested me again about half an hour later. Both times, they assured me, I "broke the record." (I've never bothered to find out if this was, in fact, the case or was something they told every patient as a method of encouraging them.) With this came comments, from both nurses and doctors, that "That's because he never smoked" and in that, I know, they were sincere. At 10 P.M. my blood gases were again measured and they were fine—oxygen level up, carbon dioxide down, and all done on my own power, without the aid of the respirator.

But then the nurse took my temperature. It was 102°. "Dr. Nolen," she said, "I'm sorry, but your temperature is still up. I'm afraid we'll have to leave the tube in overnight." I didn't cry—I couldn't with that damn tube in me—but I felt like it.

Just then Cary Akins, the chief resident, walked over. He had just gotten our of the operating room, having finished the last case, and was making final rounds in the recovery room before heading home. Cary was, as I had expected and confirmed later, the one who had opened and closed me.

"How's Dr. Nolen doing?" he asked the nurse. She showed him my breathing test results and my blood gases and then mentioned my temperature.

Cary looked down at me, then turned, and spoke to the nurse. "Suction him out one more time, then pull the tube." He looked down at me again. "I'm doing this, you know, on the assumption that you'll cough." I nodded my head in agreement. I'd promise anything, even coughing, to get rid of that damn tube.

A few minutes later, after one last vacuum-cleaning of my lungs, the tube was pulled out. "Pure bliss" is the only way to describe my feeling at that moment. (A few days later, talking to Jerry Austin, I told him how much that tube had bothered me. "That's because you did so well," he said. "If you hadn't been doing well you'd never have paid that much attention to it. We've seen that pattern often, and we know that when someone starts complaining about the tube early, it's a good sign.")

Joan came in one last time; I was shown off to her, minus my tube. She agreed later that losing the tube finally made me look as if I might live. I still wasn't able to speak to her. My vocal cords were swollen and weren't functioning well, as was to be expected, considering they'd been pushed apart by an endotracheal tube for thirteen hours. But the vocal cords recover quickly, and by 2 or 3 A.M. I was able to whisper so the nurses could understand me.

I was awake most of the rest of the night. I suppose I dozed for a few minutes after my morphine shots, but generally I remember watching the clock most of the time. The breathing and blood tests were repeated at intervals, I was asked to cough and did so to the best of my ability; and the night gradually became morning. I still hurt, but the worst of the operative experience ended for me when that endotracheal tube came out.

At 6 A.M. the resident surgeons made rounds—Cary Akins, Rick Lewis, and the rest of the staff, all looking remarkably fresh after about five hours' sleep, and after they'd checked my condition, it was decided that, unless something untoward happened, I could be moved out of the recovery room and on up to Baker 12 later in the morning. I still had a way to go before I'd be completely out of the critical period, but I had already passed the point where they felt it was necessary for me to have the intensive care the recovery room provided.

Things were looking up.

170

CHAPTER XV

July 12, 1975–July 23, 1975

When I arrived on Baker 12 (twelfth floor, Baker Building), I was assigned a corner room with a vew of Cambridge across the Charles River. Baker 12, unlike the older Phillips House, was air-conditioned. I had a pleasant, comfortable room.

While I had been in the recovery room I had, as I remember it, four plastic catheters running into arteries and veins (including the one that ran through my neck), a catheter in my bladder, and I was hooked by wires pasted onto my chest to a constant monitoring electrocardiogram. Just before I left the recovery room at about 11 A.M. two of my

171

blood-vessel lines were removed, one of which was the one in my neck.

As soon as I arrived on Baker 12, I was again hooked to a monitor. Two blood-vessel lines were kept open with intravenous fluids running constantly, since I was still pouring urine containing postassium through my catheter and the potassium had to be replaced intravenously, The day after my arrival on Baker 12, the bladder catheter and one intravenous line were removed; second day there, the last intravenous tube came out. By that time I was eating and drinking enough to keep me hydrated and they were able to replace what potassium I needed by giving me potassium salts dissolved in some sort of flavored fluid, but potassium salts no matter how they're disguised are distasteful.

The heart, once it has been operated on, has a tendency to be "irritable." Various stimuli, such as shifts in the electrolyte levels of the blood, may cause it to beat irregularly, and sometimes these irregular beats are not only inefficient but can be life-threatening. To protect against this the patient is given, every two or three or four hours, depending on dose and need, pills that are designed to reduce the irritability of the heart. So, for my first two days and nights on Baker 12, I didn't get much sleep; for one reason or another, either to check my vital signs (temperature, pulse, respiratory rate, and blood pressure) or to give me pills, it was necessary to wake me every two hours. The pain in my chest and leg incisions and a generalized soreness that affected all my muscles prevented me from dropping immediately back to sleep. So, for the first seventy-two hours after the operation, I slept only in short naps.

I spent some of my waking hours trying to figure out a schedule so that the interruptions at night might come every three rather than every two hours; once I thought I had it. Then, when I mentioned it to one of the residents he said, "It might work, but we wouldn't use it if it did. We don't like waking patients every two hours, but we think that it's just as well that we do. It means someone is checking on them. After a heart operation, a checking-over every two hours for a few days isn't a bad idea."

My temperature would occasionally bounce up to the 101 or 102 range. Then the nurse assigned to my care would "cough me out." The technique each nurse used varied with her training. One, trained in Pittsburgh, would beat a drum solo on my back with her fists to "loosen things up," as a preliminary to getting me to cough; I didn't like it, but it worked. Up would come the secretions that had collected low down in my respiratory passages and down would go my temperature.

There was also a breathing machine; a machine with a mouthpiece that I could suck on. When I did, the machine would blow air into my lungs, expanding them more than I would otherwise have done. As soon as I'd start to resist, to exhale a bit, the machine automatically shut off, so there was no possibility of it overinflating my lungs. Generally speaking, I had very minimal problems with lungs and/or breathing, which again, on several occasions and by a variety of people, was attributed to my never having smoked cigarettes.

On my third postoperative day it seemed to me that I was having more pain around my heart—not angina, just an achy feeling. I suspected that I might be getting what is known as the postpericardotomy syndrome, a mild inflammation of the pericardial sac. This condition, which causes an increased white blood cell count, elevated temperature, and chest pain, is perhaps the most common complication associated with heart surgery. It's an annoying complication, but one that usually responds nicely to cortisone or cortisonelike drugs.

I told Cary Akins about my increased discomfort. He examined me, couldn't find anything unusual and decided to take a "wait-and-see" attitude before treating me. By that evening the discomfort had diminished. It had been a false alarm, undoubtedly caused by the apprehension associated with my knowing too much about the complications of heart surgery.

Happily for me, once the catheter was removed from my bladder I had no difficulty voiding; everyone isn't so fortunate. The catheter hadn't bothered me, I was hardly conscious of it, but I was glad to be rid of it.

On Sunday, July 13, my first morning on Baker 12, I was helped out of bed at 6:30 A.M. to stand on a scale and be weighed. As I mentioned, most patients gain weight during open-heart surgery, particularly while on the pump. I was no exception. I had weighed 195 pounds on Friday morning before my operation; now, two days later, despite having poured fluid out through my bladder and having eaten almost nothing, I weighed 202; this, as I say, was expected.

Most mornings the resident surgeons began their rounds about 6:45, so that they could see all their patients and write appropriate orders before they went to the operating room or wherever it was they were to spend the day. Cary Akins, the chief resident, Chuck Hoover and/or Dave Shahein, the senoir residents, and Rich Lewis and/or Greg Scott, the junior residents, were usually in attendance. They would all stand at the foot or side of my bed and the junior resident, who had been on call the previous evening, would report, something like this:

"This is Dr. Nolen's third postoperative day. His course so far has been relatively uncomplicated. His electrocardiogram yesterday showed only an occasional extra systole [premature heartbeat of no consequence]. His potassium is 4.5 [normal]. His Foley catheter was removed yesterday and he has had no trouble voiding."

Then the senior resident would say to the charge nurse, who accompanied the residents on their morning rounds, "Diet, weight, and meds," and she would tell the residents what diet I was on (1,500 calorie, low cholesterol, low sugar), what I had weighed that morning, and what medications I was taking.

After both recitals Cary Akins or Chuck Hoover might ask a question—e.g., "Has Dr. Nolen had a postoperative chest x-ray?"—and the junior resident or the nurse, depending on who was expected to have the information, would answer. Then Cary or Chuck would issue any necessary orders—e.g., "Cut his potassium dose to three times a day," or "Be certain Dr. Nolen is out of bed at least twice a day." Then they would say good-bye and move on to the next patient.

Actually, except that they started rounds earlier, it was very much like the way we had run things at Bellevue when I was chief resident, the way, in my experience, things are run by a qualified house staff anywhere.

The EKG monitor was sort of a nuisance. I was on the wing of Baker 12, where the patients newly arrived from the recovery room were put. Each of us was on a monitor, so the continuous beeping of six or eight monitors could easily be heard in the corridors.

Any time the steady beep-beep changed, an alarm went off to summon a nurse. Supposedly, the alarm was a sign that something was wrong with the heart rate or rhythm of the patient. Of course, every time anyone's alarm went off I wondered if it might be mine, and I'd check my pulse to reassure myself. Fortunately, I developed no arrhythmia or other alarm-inducing problems in the postoperative period.

Unfortunately, however, I perspire rather easily, and repeatedly the leads that led to the monitoring EKG and were glued to my chest would come unstuck as I moved about in bed. This, too, would trip the alarm. I soon learned to stick the leads back on, when I could get them to adhere properly.

The first two days I got out of bed only to be weighed or to be "coughed out." Otherwise I stayed in bed but moved around a lot. I have never been able to sleep on my back; lying on my abdomen, with my new chest incision, was out of the question, so I turned from side to side most of the night. One of the nurses told me that putting a pillow beneath the incision in my leg would help, and it did.

By the third day I was sitting in a chair reasonably comfortably and was walking to the bathroom unaided.

Roman was in to see me every day. On about my second postoperative day, when I was ready and able to pay close attention, he told me how everything had gone. "It went very, very well," he said. "Eldy measured the flow in both grafts. Forty cc's [of blood flow per minute] is about the minimal acceptable flow; sixty is preferred. You had one hundred and twenty-five cc's a minute through the graft to your anterior descending artery and one hundred and sixty-five cc's a minute to your circumflex. It could hardly have been better."

"Any changes in my EKG?" I asked. I failed to mention earlier that in about 8 percent of patients an infarct will develop during surgery. These infarcts are generally small

176

and, for some reason, don't seem to do much significant damage to heart muscle; perhaps they are superficial. But of course it's nicer not to have one than to have one.

"No change at all," Roman said. "It looks exactly as your resting EKG did before surgery."

"I've had a lot of breaks," I said.

Roman agreed.

Eldy Mundth came to see me on my second postoperative day, and he confirmed what Roman had said.

After three days I was moved to the wing of Baker 12 where the patients who needed less attention were kept. The nurse–patient ratio at the new arrival end was about 1:2; on this end it seemed to be about 1:3. At any rate, I got all the care I seemed to need.

Jerry Austen stopped in to visit several times. We talked a little bit about my operation, but mostly about surgical training and various medical life-styles. Both of us lead what I suppose could be called "busy" lives, but completely different. And, I gathered from our conversations, neither of us would want to trade with the other.

I was now reading and making notes every day; I'd had to dictate notes to Joan for the first few postoperative days. I was still on a low-cholesterol, low-calorie diet, and was losing about 2 pounds a day. I'd sleep for longer stretches at night, and I'd nap for about an hour every morning.

On July 18, the seventh postoperative day, I was detached from the monitor. I had been temporarily unhooking myself so I could walk in the corridors, but now I tried to walk more often. I was still weak but getting stronger every day.

Father Octavio Munoz, a Catholic priest from Mexico on temporary assignment at the General, stopped in to visit every day. He was very well read and we talked mostly about books. On Saturday, the nineteenth, he said to me, "Would you like me to bring you communion tomorrow?"

"Gee, Father," I said, "I'd like that, but it's been an awful long time since I've been to confession, and I really don't know if I can honestly go, since I'm sure a lot of the things I've been doing that I'd classify as sins are things I rather expect to continue to do when I get out of here."

"Listen," he said, "are you sorry for your sins?"

"Yes," I said.

"Then I'll bring you communion tomorrow."

And he did.

I talked to some of my recuperating neighbors and listened to a variety of stories. Most seemed to have had at least one infarct before their operations, something I'd been spared. One man had had, like me, to go in through the Phillips House or else wait an extra month for admission to a less expensive bed. Two had had angina for years, but had decided on angiograms when their angina had begun to get worse. Lots of stories—no two the same but all with a common thread, chest pain—running through them.

A Dr. Ruskin, a resident in cardiology, had been a regular visitor from the day I'd first entered MGH. I liked him very much. He was always ready and willing to sit and answer questions. He was, more or less, a student of Roman's. We talked a lot about arteriosclerotic heart disease in general. We were in agreement that the eventual answer could not and would not be surgery. Surgery was not only too expensive but it didn't get to the root of the problem, prevention of the development of arteriosclerosis. Dr. Ruskin felt that in my case the most important thing for me to worry about was my blood pressure. He felt that keeping this within normal levels would do more to prevent further problems than any other single thing I might do. Roman, when I mentioned this to him, agreed.

Now I was getting restless. I felt stronger, was sick of the hospital food and rountine, and felt I could function on the outside—all signs that I was getting well. The stitches were removed from my chest incision on the tenth postoperative day (July 21). At the same time two pairs of wires, which led directly from my heart through the skin, were pulled out.

These wires were routinely left in patients who had open-heart surgery so that if the patient should develop an erratic, dangerous heartbeat in the postoperative period, an electric pacemaker could quickly be attached to the wires, directly and swiftly regulating the beat. They were left in at the time of operation as a safety measure.

Bruce Smith, another of the junior residents, was assigned the job of removing my chest stitches and the wires. He took the chest stitches out and then, as he was taking the dressings off the wires that led to my heart, said, "Once in a while these wires won't come out. They get twisted into a knot near the heart. When that happens, rather than pull too hard we just cut the wires off at skin level and let them retract beneath the skin surface. They stay in the heart, but won't do you any harm."

Frankly, I didn't at all like the idea of those wires being left behind in my heart, innocuous as they might be. I think I actually prayed as Bruce started to tug. To my great relief, the wires slid out with relative ease.

Commonly, at the General, cardiac surgical patients who have had no complications go home on the twelfth postoperative day. However, since I was going to fly back to Minnesota, Roman was reluctant to let me go so soon; he thought that Friday, the fourteenth postoperative day, might be safer.

I had a suggestion. "Why not let me out on the twenty-third, the twelfth postoperative day," I said, "but I won't fly home that day. I'll stay with Joan at the Holiday Inn and get my strength back a little, learn to live on the outside again, and fly home on Friday, the twenty-fifth. If there are any problems, I'll be close to the General and can get back in minutes."

"Fine," Roman said. "It's a deal."

The evening of the twenty-second, Roman stopped in for a final talk; he was leaving town himself and wouldn't see me on the twenty-third.

He did what every doctor should do, and most (I'm included) don't. He not only went over in detail the postoperative regimen he wanted me to follow, but wrote it all down. He also wrote down his home and office addresses and phone numbers. I have the paper tucked away in a safe place.

Basically, my regimen was to include: (1) medications to keep my blood pressure down (these might have to be adjusted as my activity increased); (2) medicines to thin my blood, i.e., anticoagulants of two types (he wasn't certain that these were necessary or helpful since the statistical study they were doing was still in progress, but he felt that the eventual results would show they were helpful); (3) increasing exercise, beginning with short walks that would become progressively longer; (4) three more weeks of abstinence from sexual activity (one's libido isn't overwhelming immediately after open-heart surgery, anyway, if my experience is typical); (5) swimming and golf in a month to six weeks; (6) six weeks more (i.e., a total of 8 weeks after surgery) before I could return to the operating room as a surgeon; and (7) I was to continue on a relatively low-cholesterol, low-sugar diet, and try to keep my weight below 185. I had entered the hospital weighing 201; I weighed 179 on the day I left.

Roman would also send a letter summarizing my hospital course, my medication, etc., to Bill Petersen, the internist who would check me about three weeks after I'd returned to Minnesota.

I also arranged to return to Massachusetts to see both Roman and Eldredth Mundth on October 23.

Bill Petersen would order interim tests—blood cholesterol and triglycerides, perhaps a repeat glucose tolerance test, and EKGs—as he felt they were indicated.

When Roman had finished, neither Joan nor I had any questions. He gave me a bag containing bottles of the medications I'd need initially, then we shook hands, I thanked him for all he'd done—words were inadequate to express the gratitude I felt—and he left.

The next day I said good-bye to the residents and nurses and at ten thirty I walked out of the Massachusetts General Hospital. I was, I knew, weaker but much healthier than the day I walked in.

Chapter XVI

Why me?

That's a question asked, I'd guess, by everyone who has ever been afflicted with a serious disease. If the patient is a child then the question—asked by parents, grandparents, sisters, or brothers—becomes why her or him.

Sometimes there's no apparent answer. Why does one ten-year-old little boy develop bone cancer, while none of his playmates do; why does this young woman have leukemia, while her friends are healthy; why should this middle-aged man suffer from severe asthma, when none of his relatives or friends have it? Perhaps, as our knowledge of medicine increases, the answers to these questions, which aren't apparent now, will become clear, even obvious.

As soon as I became a patient I asked the same question, Why me? But with heart disease, although we don't have all the answers for everyone, we do have some answers. When I look back on my life I can see at least a few of the reasons why I developed the disease when others of my contemporaries didn't.

To say that coronary artery disease is common is a gross understatement. In fact, if you break down the causes of death into age groups and subdivide them again according to sex and color, here is the way coronary artery disease would rank:

Age	White male	White female	Black male	Black female
25–29	Fourth	Sixth	Third	Fifth
30–34	Second	Fifth	Second	First
35–39	First	First	Second	First
40–44	First	First	First	First
45–49	First	First	First	First
45–49	First	First	First	First
50–54	First	First	First	First
55–59	First	First	First	First
60–64	First	First	First	First
65–69	First	First	First	First
70–74	First	First	First	First

No one knows with certainty why blacks are even more susceptible to coronary artery disease than are whites, but it's obvious there's more than enough of the disease for both races.

Coronary artery disease seems to be related to at least

184

nine factors: sex, genetics, personality, cigarette smoking, blood pressure, stress, weight, diet, and exercise habits. The correlation with some of these factors is well established; with others, less so. We have at least some control over all but the first two. Let's consider them one at a time.

Sex : Women are not as susceptible to coronary-artery disease as men are. The difference is largely due to estrogen, the female hormone, which delays the development of arteriosclerosis.

But once the menopause has begun, women become progressively more susceptible. Until the age of forty-five men have thirteen times as many heart attacks as women. Between forty-five and sixty-two, men have twice as many. After sixty-two, the incidence is about the same.

Genetics : If you want longevity, it helps to be the child of parents who lived into their nineties. There is evidence that the sons of men who had coronary-artery disease tend to develop the disease at an earlier age than their fathers. But if your father died of a heart attack at age forty-five, don't despair. Admittedly, you may be more coronary-prone than the average person, but we have learned a lot about heart disease since your father died; if he had had the information and the medicine available to you, he might have lived much longer.

Still, if coronary-artery disease has been prevalent in your family, it behooves you to pay particular heed to the other factors, those that are within your control.

Personality : It's possible, using psychological testing, to divide people into two groups, type A and type B. Type A people are those who are aggressive, competitive, and very time-conscious; if you're the sort of person who is compulsively punctual, who has his day and evening precisely

185

planned, who never seems to have enough time to do all the things he wants to do, you're definitely a type A.

Type Bs are those who seem never to be in a hurry, who aren't continually competing for raises or promotions, who don't mind putting things off for another day. Type Bs are the naturally relaxed people.

Some people don't fit clearly into either group, but most have characteristics that allow them to be classified as either A or B.

Well-controlled studies done over several years have shown that type A people are at least twice as likely to develop coronary-artery disease as are type Bs.

Unfortunately, it isn't safe to conclude from this study that if you are a type A person and if you manage to relax more and not be so competitive (possibly by using tranquilizers; I'm definitely a type A and I can't think of any other method that would work with me) that you would then become a type B, and less prone to heart disease. Possibly this is so but no study has ever been done to show it.

It seems more likely that type As and type Bs are genetically determined and that superficial personality changes won't change their tendency to get or not to get heart disease.

My own opinion is that if you're a type A it's worthwhile to make some effort to relax more; but I wouldn't worry much about making a radical change in your personality that may well be futile. Concentrate on the other things you can do that will definitely help prevent coronary-artery disease from developing.

Smoking: The risk of a heavy cigarette smoker's dying of heart disease is three times as high as for the nonsmoker. (Heavy cigar and pipe smokers don't have an increased incidence of heart disease, though there are, of course, other health risks that they run.)

Blood pressure: This is one factor over which each of us has much more control than our parents or grandparents did. And it's important. Many studies show that the incidence of heart attacks is three times higher in patients with elevated blood pressure than it is in those with normal blood pressure.

Thirty years ago, if you suffered from high blood pressure, your doctor would tell you to lose weight and cut down on salt; probably he'd prescribe a mild sedative. If those things didn't work, you'd just have to live with your high blood pressure.

Weight loss, salt restriction, and sedatives are still helpful; but if they don't bring your blood pressure down to normal, your doctor has many other safe and effective drugs he can prescribe. These days, no one with high blood pressure should go untreated.

Stress: A man who drives a cab in mid-Manhattan is more likely to develop coronary-artery disease than is a man who earns his living as a gardener. A business executive, fighting his way up the corporate ladder, is more coronary-prone than a librarian. Emotional stress raises blood pressure, elevates cholesterol, and contributes to the incidence of heart attacks.

If you are a high-coronary-risk type for any reason, then you would do well to stay away from situations that put you under a great deal of constant stress.

But remember that frustration is also a form of stress. The gardener who is discontented with his lot is under more stress than the business executive who is happy in his competitive career.

Weight: No one knows whether excess weight is a direct cause of heart disease, but we do know that being overweight may cause an increase in both your blood pressure and blood cholesterol. So, at least indirectly, excess weight contributes to coronary-artery disease.

We also know that the mortality rate from all causes is higher for fat people than it is for thin people. For example, women who are 30 percent overweight have a 30 percent higher mortality rate than those of normal weight. For a man who is 20 percent overweight, the mortality rate increases by 50 percent.

Diet: This is a very controversial problem, one for which we certainly don't have all the answers.

There are, for example, many doctors who feel very strongly that a high-cholesterol diet markedly increases the chance that an individual will develop heart disease. This seems to be a reasonable theory; after all, arteriosclerotic plaques are composed largely of cholesterol. And statistically, other factors being equal, people who run consistently high blood-cholesterol levels are at least three times as likely to have heart attacks as are those with low-cholesterol levels.

But, unfortunately, no matter how reasonable the theory sounds, there really isn't any incontrovertible evidence that low-cholesterol diets do in fact protect patients from heart disease, even if the diet is so low in cholesterol that it reduces blood cholesterol, and such diets are not very palatable and rarely adhered to.

A recent study, done by doctors at the University of Minnesota, involved seventeen thousand state hospital patients, chosen because their diets could be closely controlled. Half the patients ate standard normal diets, the other half ate low-cholesterol diets. Four and a half years later the researchers added up the number of heart attacks, strokes, and other heart and blood vessel problems that had afflicted each group. The doctor who reported on the survey at a November, 1975, meeting of the American Heart Association said, "In the entire population including men and women of all ages over twenty-one, despite a satisfactory decrease in blood cholesterol there was not the slightest hint of benefit." He also added, "I still believe in the theory, but it's awfully hard to demonstrate."

Similar results have been obtained in other, even more comprehensive, studies. One particularly intriguing study was reported in *The Relaxation Response* by Dr. Herbert Benson. This was a study done on a group of veterans, some of whom ate a low-cholesterol diet while the others ate a normal diet. After five years a re-evaluation of the two groups showed, as might be expected, that the incidence of heart disease was lower in the group that ate a low-cholesterol diet. Unfortunately, the overall mortality from all causes was higher in the low-cholesterol group than in the other group. Not a very encouraging study.

The fact is that cholesterol metabolism varies among races and even among individuals. Some people can eat high-cholesterol diets without raising their blood-cholesterol level; others can't. Some people can tolerate high blood-cholesterol levels; others can't. and much of the cholesterol that gets into our blood is manufactured in our body and is essential to smooth functioning of the brain and other organs. Without cholesterol, we couldn't live.

Triglycerides are other fatty substances normally found in the blood. Laboratory techniques that enable us to measure triglycerides accurately have been generally available only for about five years, so we don't as yet have many long-term studies on the effects of triglycerides on the heart and blood vessels, but preliminary evidence is suggestive. Some studies show that individuals who chronically run high blood-triglyceride levels seem to be particularly susceptible to coronary-artery disease. However, there are other very recent studies that show absolutely no correlation between blood-triglyceride levels and coronary-artery disease. Obviously we have much to learn.

Triglyceride metabolism is even more confusing than that of cholesterol. Normal triglyceride levels run between 60 and 150 milligrams per 100 cc of blood. As with cholesterol, much of our triglycerides are manufactured in the body, but diet also affects the level. In some people, cholesterol in the diet raises the blood-triglyceride level; in others, sugar or alcohol will trigger an increase. And some triglycerides are apparently harmless while others may be dangerous. A special blood test, electrophoresis, must be done to tell which sort of triglycerides are in a patient's blood.

Fortunately, if I use sugar substitutes, eat a moderately low-cholesterol diet, and avoid drinking an excessive amount of alcohol—excessive meaning more than three drinks an evening—my triglyceride levels stay at about 200 mgms per 100 cc of blood. Upper level of normal for triglycerides is usually about 150 mg. per 100 cc, so 200 isn't too bad. If I were to eat two pieces of cake and drink half a dozen scotch and sodas (an ugly combination) my triglyceride would zoom to the 600–1200 level. So you'll understand why I now watch my sugar, cholesterol, alcohol intake. (On the one occasion when I was on a rigid low-sugar, low-cholesterol, no-alcohol diet for three weeks, my blood triglyceride still didn't drop below 200. For me, that is apparently as low as it gets. Which in one way is disappointing—I wish it was about 60 or 70. But, in another way, it's consoling to know that total abstinence doesn't do any good. I don't feel guilty every time I take a drink.)

There are drugs that will lower blood cholesterol and or triglyceride. Chlorfibrate, d-thyroxine (a thyroid hormone), and nicotinic acid are the three most widely used. Unfortunately, none of them works on every individual and all may be associated with annoying side effects. Chlorfibrate is the most reliable and, under the trade name of Atromid-S, is most widely used. Unfortunately, it is also a drug associated with many side effects. And, according to the description of the drug in the literature that accompanies the medicine, "It has not been established whether the drug-induced lowering of serum cholesterol or lipid (fat) levels has a detrimental, beneficial, or no effect on the morbidity or mortality due to atherosclerosis or coronary artery disease."

With a disclaimer like that—a realistic disclaimer, I might add—it should be apparent why doctors resort to drug treatment only when they must.

In summary we can safely say that, given a choice between running high or low blood-cholesterol and/or triglyceride levels, it would be reasonable to choose low. It's probably best, for those who run high levels, to avoid eating foods that help to cause elevations of either. But, remember, just because you do run high blood-fat levels does not mean you are going to get heart disease. Nor is there any irrefutable evidence that rigidly depriving yourself of all the good things you like to eat and drink is going to protect you from disease.

With the knowledge we now have—and to me it seems likely that this will continue to be the case—moderation seems, as it so often does, to be the best policy.

Finally, let's consider vitamins. I'd guess that every year there is enough money spent on vitamin supplements to provide an adequate diet for the starving people of Bangladesh. At least 99 percent of this money is wasted.

Anyone who eats even a relatively normal diet will, without making any effort, get all the vitamins he or she needs. Any vitamin intake above the minimum requirement is either excreted from the body or stored in body fat, where it sits, not serving any purpose. Anytime someone has claimed that a vitamin or a combination of vitamins will cure some ailment—heart disease, impotency, and aging are three popular targets—controlled studies done by qualified scientists have shown that the claims can't be substantiated.

You'd expect, when the claims for vitamins are disproved, that people would stop wasting their money on vitamin supplements. That would be the reasonable result of the research. But people are not always reasonable. They will simply not accept these reports, well-documented as they are. They go right on eating vitamins that, for all the good they're doing, might just as well be flushed down a drain.

Personally, I've given up trying to talk people out of taking vitamins. I tell them, "It's your money; if you want to waste it, that's your privilege." Only rarely does anyone go to such an excess that he or she manages to produce vitamin toxicity; at that point, it's usually possible to persuade the victim to kick the vitamin habit.

In our culture, vitamin capsules function in the place of

the charms that witch doctors used to give to their patients to ward off disease.

Exercise: I've put this last, but it is certainly not the least. In fact, I consider exercise the most important factor of all. Why? Exercise lowers blood cholesterol and blood pressure, helps control weight, and relieves stress and tension. It keeps your body as a whole healthy.

It is also good for the heart. The heart is basically a muscular organ, and like any other muscle it becomes flabby with disuse. Exercise it regularly—not with isometrics, which are of questionable value, but by walking, jogging, playing tennis, swimming, or some other other strenuous activity—and it will stay in good shape. People who exercise regularly have only one-third as many heart attacks as those who don't exercise; and if they do have a coronary, their chances of surviving it are vastly increased. A well-exercised heart has more reserve than a flabby one.

All the factors that contribute to coronary-artery disease (again excepting sex and genetics) are interrelated. That's what makes it so difficult to evaluate the relative importance of each. For example, if you compare ten men with high blood cholesterol to ten with normal blood cholesterol, you have to be certain that they are all of normal weight and normal blood pressure, with similar occupations and smoking habits, before you can attribute any difference in the incidence of heart attacks solely to the cholesterol. Finding groups like these and eliminating variables have and always will be difficult.

Now, you may well ask, if I know so much about heart disease, why did I get into trouble? Where did I go wrong?

First, there wasn't much I could do about my genetic background; I do come, on the male side, from a family where heart disease has been prevalent. But I should have planned on being one of the susceptible males instead of assuming that because my face looked like my mother's my heart would look like hers, too. I should have been more attentive to the factors I could control.

High on that list would have to be my blood pressure. High blood pressure and cigarette smoking are two factors in which the statistical linkage to coronary-artery disease are very definite; I never smoked cigarettes. (How many times have I bragged about that in writing this book? You cigarette smokers are going to hate me.) On the other hand, I never paid as much attention to my blood pressure as I should have.

Admittedly, in 1953 when I first learned that, like my father, I had labile hypertension (labile means it bounces around a lot; sometimes it's high, sometimes it isn't) there wasn't much available in the way of treatment. But since about 1955 there have been drugs available that worked reasonably well. Admittedly, some people simply couldn't tolerate the side effects of the available medications, so they chose to give them up. But since 1960—and particularly since 1970 —there have been so many effective drugs to choose from that almost anyone who really worked at it, with the help of a physician who knew and cared, could bring his or her blood pressure down to reasonable levels without suffering intolerable side effects.

I didn't take advantage of this opportunity. I've taken pills for my blood pressure fairly regularly since about 1963, but I refused to check at regular intervals to see if the pills were doing the job. If I had my blood pressure checked once and it was at an acceptable level, I might not have it checked again for a year or more. I hated to take more pills and I was always afraid a recheck would show that I needed more medication. So I practically ignored my blood pressure.

Three years ago I finally started taking two kinds of pills twice a day. This brought my blood pressure, which had gotten up into the 180/100 range, down to about 150/90; it was still high, but marginally so, and I was willing to accept it.

Then one day (or night) I didn't get an erection when I wanted and expected one. Naturally, the first thing I did was to quit one of my blood pressure pills, one that I knew sometimes caused impotence. Given a choice between normal blood pressure and impotency and high blood pressure and potency, I'd take the latter every time. (I still would.)

What I should have realized was that transient impotence—and it was very transient—was, possibly, not due to the pill but just one of those things that happens occasionally to the best of us. Instead I stayed off the pill for about a year till my elevated blood pressure finally scared me back onto it, without, I might add, any recurrence of the impotence.

To put it succinctly, when it came to blood pressure control, I behaved like an idiot. I might add here that my doctors let me get away with this. Instead of chewing me out, insisting I take better care of myself—as they would have if I were a layman—they let me guide myself. Another example of that very common phenomenon—the doctor who doesn't always get optimum medical care.

I exercised regularly and vigorously—I can't be faulted there—but I did let my weight sneak up on me. I weighed 176 when I came to Litchfield in 1960. Every three years since then I've gained about five pounds, hardly perceptible, really, or so I thought (and others assured me)—till I got on a scale. Scales don't lie.

I shouldn't have let that happen. As we get older, our metabolism slows down and to maintain a steady weight we have to cut back on our food intake. I didn't, so I put on weight that probably contributed to the increase in my blood pressure. (Actually, as I've learned since my operation, there's no "probably" about it. I've kept my weight between 170 and 175 since the operation and my blood pressure, though I'm taking only two pills a day as opposed to the six a day I was on when I went to the hospital, has remained normal. I was up to 180/100 when I entered MGH; I'm at 120–30/80–84 now. Admittedly, I'm not really under any stress yet; but when I weighed 195, even when I was at rest or on vacation my blood pressure never dropped to normal.)

My eating habits—the kinds of food I eat as well as the quantity—are probably open to criticism, but I really don't feel very guilty about them. My cholesterol levels have, on the few occasions they've been checked, been within normal levels; and medical concern over tryglycerides is really fairly recent, so I don't feel guilty about not working at keeping my tryglycerides low. I've always felt that the health-food faddists don't really know what they're talking about. Actually, I've yet to see any solid evidence that would lend credibility to claims they've made. I do feel, however, as I mentioned earlier, that those who should keep their cholesterol intakes low deserve a better break than they are now getting in restaurants and fast-food chains in the United States. I am one of the lucky ones who can eat a moderate amount of cholesterol-soaked food without raising my blood-cholesterol level, but some people can't. Restaurateurs ought to realize that there are people who are hurt by eating the foot that dominates their menus. They ought to offer, along with the rich sauces and fatty beef, a choice of low-cholesterol items for the man or woman who can't safely eat the other items on the menu. Fair is fair.

It would be nice, for example, if restaurants would offer patrons a choice between margarine and butter; between cholesterol-free or regular mayonnaise; between regular salt or a salt substitute. It would be an easy thing for restaurants to do, a service that could be added with minimal inconvenience. But it will only be done if restaurant patrons demand it, just as it was patron demand that finally made restaurants start offering caffeine-free coffee as an alternative to regular coffee. I am certain that the patron demand for low-cholesterol food exists; whether it will ever be organized well enough to effect any changes is, I admit, questionable. Perhaps we can get a Ralph Nader group to work on it.

Though I think a case can and should be made for having these low-cholesterol foods available in restaurants, let me emphasize that I am not, by any stretch of the imagination, a health-food addict. I have read all the articles I can find on nutrition—not just the medical literature, but the books and pamphlets published by the health-food cultists—and have never found one iota of evidence to suggest that eating the so-called natural foods peddled by health-food promoters adds one second to one's longevity or well-being. The best that can be said for the food cultists is that while they are running around seeking out natural foods, they are at least staying out of trouble. They have an innocuous hobby that will neither help nor hurt them, which is more than can be said for some other pursuits.

As far as alcohol is concerned, I like it. In the past, on more occasions than I like to admit to, I've drunk more than I should have and suffered through horrible hangovers the next day. But usually, I think, I've used alcohol with moderation and enjoyed it. I don't want to quit drinking and I don't intend to. The dietitian at the MGH told me in one of our instruction meetings that the usual drink equals in caloric content a slice of bread and butter. I'm willing to pass up my bread and butter ration.

Finally, stress. I wrote earlier a capsule summary of what my life-style is like. Some of my friends, co-workers, and family said, when they first heard I had a heart problem, "no wonder. Look at the pace at which he's been living." I plead guilty, but with qualifications.

What one person finds strenuous, another can manage with ease. For the insurance man, it would certainly be stressful to have to take out an appendix; performing an appendectomy doesn't stress me at all. On the other hand, if someone handed me an insurance policy and said, "Here, go ring that doorbell and try to sell this to the occupant," my blood pressure would probably go right off the top of the meter. Selling is something I would find very stressful.

I don't think that either practicing surgery or writing are sources of stress for me, except when I get overcommitted so that I have difficulty finding time to accomplish everything to which I've obligated myself. The overcommitment trap is one a lot of us fall into. I'm going to do my best to avoid it in the future, though I'm sure that, once in a while, I'll get caught again. I think anyone who expects to accomplish anything has to be prepared to live with some stress. To me, life without some stress would not be attractive.

One thing I am giving up is public speaking. I've never enjoyed it, even though it pays reasonably well (my wife has never understood why anyone would pay so much to hear me talk, and I agree); and even though, like most people who wander around the country lecturing, I have a fifty-minute lecture that I can rattle off almost without thinking and feel reasonably certain it will be well liked. This speech will also, with minimal modification, fit any of the six or seven different titles from which the hiring group has made a choice.

Nevertheless, the mere thought of driving to the airport, flying to the meeting of one or another organization, having lunch or dinner, speaking, visiting, staying in a motel, and flying back the next day exhausts me. I have resigned from my speaking agency.

Radio, television, and newspaper interviews, all of which are helpful in selling books, are not a source of stress for me. Someone asks a question and I either answer it or say, "I don't know." I don't find that strenuous and I will, when it seems appropriate, continue to make these appearances. (After all, if you write a book you want to sell it.)

Overall, as I look back on my first forty-seven years and ask, "Why me?" I can see rather clearly some of the reasons I ran into trouble. If I had it to do again I'd repeat most of it, but I'll concede that I'd have done a few things differently.

But in this life we don't always get second chances. Who knows, perhaps that's just as well.

CHAPTER XVII

July 23, 1975–July 26, 1975

Joan and I walked the block and a half between the General and the Holiday Inn. By the time we got to our room I was tired. This was just a little bit farther than I'd walked while in the hospital.

I flopped down on my bed in the room, read the paper, and relaxed. Everyone had been nice to me at General but it was pleasant to be out and on my own. Some people who spend a long time in the hospital, a month or more, get what we call hospitalitis; they don't want to or are afraid to leave. They feel safe and secure in the hospital. I'd been in no danger of catching that "disease."

By eleven thirty, after a half hour on the bed, I was ready

to move. Joan had been eating lunch each day at whatever sandwich shop happened to be near so I said, "How about it? Shall we grab a cab out to Jimmy's Harborside [a well-known seafood restaurant with a nice view of the ocean] and celebrate with a decent lunch?"

"Do you feel up to it?" she asked.

"I think so," I said. "Shouldn't really be any strain."

So we caught a cab for the ten-minute ride. We got there early, about eleven forty-five, and there wasn't any crowd. Joan had a bloody Mary and scallops; I had a bottle of beer and baked scrod. After the hospital food, which had been adequate but boring, the lunch was a welcome change.

I took a nap when we got back to the motel and that evening we went to a movie, *The Invitation,* an excellent French film. Then we went to Stella's for dinner. When I had been a medical student in Boston (1949–53), Stella's was a plain, inexpensive Italian restaurant in the North End of Boston and I ate there almost every Sunday night. Now Stella's is on the ocean near the aquarium, fancier, and more expensive. But their linguini with clam sauce is still excellent.

We were back at the motel at ten thirty and I went right to bed and to sleep. I was tired, but not overly so.

Thursday my sister Mary drove up from Connecticut and Chappie came down from Portsmouth. We had a lot of laughs together; they're both naturally happy people and fun to be around. When they'd gone I took a nap, then sat in the sun by the pool for an hour. We had dinner that evening with Walker Connor, an old friend from my high school days, one of the few with whom I've kept in touch. He is now a professor of international relations at a college in New York but was visiting colleagues in Harvard. We talked about our high school days, naturally, and about our plans. He had a Woodrow Wilson fellowship and all next year would be in Washington, D.C., lecturing and doing research on a book he's writing. We had dinner at a Chinese restaurant near the motel, and he then left about 9 P.M. for Vermont, where he and his family spend the summer.

Joan and I stayed in, read, and went to bed early.

I've mentioned my activities on my first two days out of the hospital, not because they were particularly fascinating (except to me) but because they should make it clear that—though they were my twelfth and thirteenth postoperative days, still relatively early in the recovery period—I felt very well and was able to be reasonably active without getting tired. (I will have to admit that I tried twice to walk to a bookstore about four blocks from the motel, and both times I turned back, too tired to make it. The four blocks, however, were all uphill.)

On Friday we didn't do much but walk around the streets near the motel and sit in the sun near the pool. We caught the 4:50 P.M. nonstop flight to Minneapolis, getting into the Minneapolis airport, where our three girls met us at about 7 P.M.

One comment on the plane trip. The airline offered two entrées, beef covered with gravy or fish covered with a cream sauce. On my two days of eating out before I left Boston, I had gone off my diet—I felt I deserved a reward—but now I was back on it. All I could eat on the plane was the salad and even then I had to eat it without dressing.

(I've long wanted to ask a couple of questions about food on planes: Why do they serve so much and why, when sugar is so expensive, is a piece of cake or some other dessert invariably served with the meal and, almost invariably, dumped in the garbage with one or no bites taken out of it? Airline meals are both wasteful and fattening.)

On the way from the airport back to Litchfield we stopped at Lund's, a food store well-known in the Minneapolis area because it carries a wide variety of foods. We picked up some low-cholesterol foods that I was afraid (correctly, as it turned out) wouldn't be available in Litchfield. I'd heard of the fake eggs, of course—I think Arthur Godfrey told me about them—but Lund's carried a lot of foods I hadn't even known existed. We bought, among other things, cheese made out of skim milk (99 percent fat-free), cholesterol-free mayonnaise, artificial sweeteners, and cottage cheese that contained only 2 percent butterfat. I'm sure if we had stayed longer (we were both anxious to get home) we could have found many other foods of a similar sort, there or in a health-food store.

We arrived home in Litchfield—a wonderful feeling—at 8:30 P.M. That night we slept in town, visiting with our children, and the next day, Saturday, after I'd stopped at the clinic to say hello to the nurses and my partners, we drove out to the lake and I started writing this book. It was certainly nice to be home.

As you might imagine, when I got back to Litchfield a lot of people, men and their wives, wanted to know about my operation, not solely because of their interest in me but because they wondered if they might have something the matter with their hearts.

After all, I looked and acted like a very healthy forty-seven-year-old man right up through the day I left Litchfield to have an operation on my heart. There were and are a lot of my contemporaries in Litchfield and everywhere else who don't look or act as well as I did and yet, as far as they know (a very critical point) they don't have heart trouble. Should they be worrying about that possibility? Should they, perhaps, be doing something about it?

I've tried in this book to make it clear that all the answers aren't in yet. It's possible that a year from now one or both of my blood vessels will have shut down. I certainly hope that won't happen—I don't expect that it will happen—but I have to be realistic and recognize that the possibility exists.

The coronary by-pass operation is *an* answer to coronary-artery disease. For many people it's the best answer we have at the moment and probably the best we'll have for many years. It's certainly far better than anything we've had to offer patients with coronary-artery disease in the past. But the final solution to coronary-artery disease will come only when we find a way to prevent the development of arteriosclerosis.

In the meantime, what about those people we hear and read about time and time again, those individuals—usually males between the ages of thirty-five and fifty-five—who suddenly and unexpectedly drop dead of heart attacks while playing golf, shoveling snow, or just carrying on their businesses? Is there anything that can and should be done to prevent these deaths?

A friend of mine, a forty-seven-year-old man I'll call Ralph, told me that he had recently gone to his doctor complaining of chest pain. Ralph had a fairly strong family history of heart disease. He had also had, for at least ten years, a persistently elevated blood-cholesterol level.

"My doctor examined me," Ralph said, "took my blood pressure, listened to my heart, even took an EKG. He told me everything was fine.

" 'How about this chest pain I get?' " I asked him.

" 'It comes on only when you run, is that right?' " the doctor asked.

I said, "Yes."

" 'Then don't run,' the doctor told me. "So I don't, and I don't have any more chest pain."

This is not a spectacularly atypical example of the fatalistic approach many doctors take to possible coronary-artery disease. Ralph seemed to think he had been given sound advice; I, naturally, disagree.

The advice I give my concerned friends is this:

First, if you aren't getting regular, strenuous physical exercise, you should be. It's the best medicine there is for your heart.

This doesn't mean that if you've been doing nothing but sitting around getting fat for five years that you ought to immediately go out to the track and try to run a four-minute mile. It means that you ought to go to your doctor, have a general physical checkup, and then under his direction begin an exercise regimen that will with time lead to a routine in which you are regularly giving your whole body—including your heart—a workout. Running or swimming are particularly valuable forms of exercise.

If you are already getting regular vigorous exercise, the kind that raises your pulse rate to 130 or more, or if you eventually work up to that level, and if you have no symptoms that suggest angina, then you really don't need a formal stress test. You are giving yourself one every time you exercise.

If, as you increase your exercise and your pulse/rate to the level your doctor feels you should reach, and you have anginal pains (or pain you think might be angina), then your doctor will probably suggest, as mine did, that you have a stress electrocardiogram done. I'd go along with that suggestion—and with the subsequent angiogram and operation, if necessary. I can say this with certainty, since it's the course I followed.

Across the medical spectrum you will find physicians who are more medically oriented than I am, less convinced the by-pass operation has been proved valuable. I've already given some of the reasons they offer for a more conservative approach. You'll also find surgeons much more aggressive than I am.

For example, there is in the United States one well-known cardiac surgeon who takes a treadmill with him whenever he is invited to speak to a group of businessmen. After his lecture he gives a treadmill test to any men in the audience who want one. It has even been reported that on one occasion, after a businessman flunked his stress test, the surgeon flew the businessman back with him to his hospital, got an angiogram, and operated on the man within the week. This surgeon argues, "If we're going to prevent seven hundred thousand patients from dying of heart attacks every year, we've got to be aggressive." He may be right, but he'll need more data before most doctors will accept his aggressive approach.

However, let us assume you have had a heart attack—a myocardial infarction—and have now recovered, are up and about, back to work and your usual preinfarct activity and are not having any angina. Should an angiogram be done to see what condition your coronary arteries are in?

I suspect that some doctors would say, "No," feeling that unless the patient has angina, there is no point in having an angiogram done.

I would disagree. I would, of course, have to know the particular patient and his history before making a specific recommendation, but generally if the heart attack struck without any previous warning, i.e., if the patient had no angina prior to his infarction, then it would seem only logical to assume that he might have another infarction again without any premonitory angina. This has, in fact, been the history of many patients who have had two or more infarcts. I know that if I had had an infarction that had come on without warning, I would want, once I'd recovered—assuming no specific contraindication existed—to have an angiogram done to determine whether I was a candidate for a coronary by-pass operation. And—though I know other doctors would disagree—this is what I would tell any patient who sought my advice.

We need continuing studies because, and this needs emphasis, neither I nor anyone else can say that the man who is living a sedentary life and continues to do so will die of a heart attack. I have plenty of friends in my own age group who never get any strenuous physical exercise. Their coronary arteries may be perfectly clean or they may be nearly shut down by arteriosclerotic plaques. These men may live to be ninety and die quietly of what we call old age. Or, they may end like those whose obituaries we read every day: Mr. John Smith, forty-eight, died suddenly while eating dinner in his home. Death was attributed to a heart attack." Unless an individual is eager to find out whether he has heart disease we can't predict which group he'll be in. As Chip Gold said to me the evening after my angiogram, when I was a bit down, "Look, Bill, the only difference between you and me may be that you know what you've got."

Not everyone is eager to know—or to test—his or her

208

hearts. Some men have no taste for vigorous exercise. It is certainly their privilege to choose a sedentary life-style.

I have always lived an active life; I might have chosen to reduce my activities and might have lived comfortably for another twenty years. The odds were against this, but it was a possibility.

I chose, instead, to undergo an operation and to change certain aspects of my life-style so that I could continue to lead the active life I so much enjoy.

I have no intention of insisting that any other man do as I did. I think only that every man has the right when he makes a choice to have it be an informed one.

That is why I have written this book.

After I had left the hospital, while I was recuperating, a friend of mine who practices cardiac surgery put me in touch with other patients who had had their by-pass operations earlier than mine. I called some of them, introduced myself, and asked them to tell me about their experiences. Here are some representative histories.

(1) Mr. B.L., a farmer, is sixty-seven years old.

"In 1967, when I was fifty-nine, I had a heart attack and was in the hospital for three weeks. I got over that one and went back to farming; I've got a two hundred and forty-acre farm and I milk eighty cows. But I guess I overdid it because a year later I had another attack and was in the hospital again for another three weeks.

"I got over this one and went back to work. I started a little slower this time but now I noticed that any time I tried to do anything real hard—pitch hay or even carry milk cans—I'd get pains in my chest. I'd never had pains in my chest before. Both my heart attacks had come on real suddenly.

"At first the pains would only begin when I worked very hard, and they'd go away when I stopped, but after about three months it got so I could hardly do anything—even walk fast—without having trouble. And it took longer for the pain to go away. My doctor thought my electrocardiogram looked okay, considering I'd had two heart attacks, but he finally sent me to a heart specialist. He did a stress electrocardiogram but even after that was done he couldn't be sure what I had, so he said I should have an angiogram. That showed blocks in two of the big arteries in the front part of my heart.

"It was May of 1971 by now and I was sixty-three years old. That's when I had my operation. They sewed veins from my leg to the two blocked arteries. I was out of bed after three days, home in ten days, and back running the farm in three months."

"How have you been over the four years since the operation?" I asked.

"Fine," he said. "Never have a bit of trouble. I still run the operation pretty much by myself, though lately I've been thinking of selling out and moving to town. I'm sixty-seven, you know, and it's time that me and Mother took a little vacation. These cows tie a man down. With the price of farm land where it is now, we could live pretty comfortably for a long while."

"Are you pleased with the results of the operation?" I asked.

"I couldn't be happier," he said. "You know, I had a younger brother who died in 1958 at the age of forty-five.

Had a heart attack and went that same day. It's too bad this operation wasn't around back then."

(2) Mr. D.R. is fifty-eight. He is a business executive who is president and owner of his own hospital supply company.

"I've always worked pretty hard," he said. "I'm one of those type A people, I guess. Six years ago, in December of 1969 when I was fifty-two, I was sitting in the office one night—I usually work two nights a week—when I got a tight feeling in my chest. Sort of a choking feeling, as if I couldn't get my breath. I grabbed one of the oxygen machines we have here and breathed that for about five minutes and I felt okay. I went home, went to bed, and the next day I called my doctor and told him what had happened. I went to his office and had an electrocardiogram, which was perfectly normal. He gave me some pills and I went home.

"A few days later I had a second attack, about like the first but not quite so bad. I called my doctor again and this time, even though the electrocardiogram was normal, I had a stress test done. That was positive—lots of changes as soon as I started to exercise. He put me in the hospital, got some tests, and had me stay quiet for a week. I had a few minor attacks but now they knew what was wrong, so I'd get a nitroglycerine tablet when one began and that would relieve me.

"When all the blood tests were done, my doctor called in a heart surgeon. He advised an angiogram and I agreed to it. It was done the last week in December and it showed that two of the arteries to my heart were almost completely blocked. He advised an operation and I agreed. I knew I couldn't go on long with these attacks.

211

"The operation was done on January 4, 1970. Unfortunately, I got a staph infection in my chest incision so I had to stay in the hospital for three weeks. When I went home I was on antibiotics for two more months. Then, in March, about three months after my operation, I went back to the hospital and they took out the wire stitches they had used to sew my sternum back together. Shortly after that the wounds stopped draining."

"How have you been since the operation?" I asked.

"Couldn't be better," he answered. "Haven't had a bit of pain since they took those wires out. I had a repeat angiogram in January of 1971, a year after the operation, and it showed that both grafts were wide open. I still work two nights a week and I hike, do yard work, and play golf on weekends. I really should go back for another checkup, I suppose; I haven't seen my doctor for three years. But I feel so great I don't really think it's necessary."

Mr. D.R.'s case makes it clear that all patients who undergo open-heart surgery don't recover as rapidly and smoothly as I did. When I became a candidate for surgery I was, except for my blocked coronary arteries, in excellent condition. Because I had exercised regularly and was not markedly overweight, my body tolerated the stress of the operation very well. Patients who have let themselves go, who have lived sedentary lives and are grossly overweight, may develop postoperative complications and require a longer period of gradual rehabilitation before they get back to full activity. But, as the mortality figures demonstrate, the vast majority do eventually recover and return to active productive life. It is hoped that if they learn a lesson from their operation, they'll live more sensibly after their operations than they did before.

212

(3) Mr. D.K. is a stockbroker. He is forty-seven years old.

"In October of 1972, a little more than three years ago, I was grouse hunting with two of my sons when our jeep got stuck in the mud. We had to push pretty hard to get it out and when I got home that night I had an aching feeling in my chest. I assumed I'd strained a muscle.

"The next day the pain was still there so I called my doctor. Just to be safe, he had me come in and he did an EKG, which was perfectly normal. He thought I might just have an upset stomach and he gave me some pills to take. The pain went away a day later.

"But then, about a week later after a tough day at the office the pain came back and this time it ran from my chest into both my arms. I called my doctor again and he put me in the hospital. The electrocardiogram was still normal but he called in a cardiologist and he suggested an angiogram."

"Didn't they do a stress test first?" I asked.

"No," Mr. D.K. answered. "They thought I should have an angiogram right away. I don't know why. Anyway, I agreed and a couple of days later it was done. It showed that one artery was ninety percent closed and another was eighty-five percent closed. The angiogram was done on a Friday, and on Saturday they told me they thought I should have an operation, and that if I wanted, the heart surgeon had some open time on Monday and I could have it then. I agreed, and I'm sure glad I did. Some friends of mine have had to wait three or four weeks for their operations and they were nervous wrecks by the time they got to them.

"The operation went fine. I was up on the third day and home on the tenth. Actually, the worst part for me was just before I went home when my doctor told me they wanted to

213

do another angiogram just to make sure the grafts were open. I was afraid they'd find something wrong, but they didn't; both grafts were wide open. Just a month ago [in October, 1975] I had a stress test that was perfect.''

"You must be pleased with the result," I said.

"I certainly am," he replied. "I was back at work eight weeks after the operation and I haven't had a sick day since. I went grouse hunting with my kids again this fall.

"My father had his first heart attack at the age of forty-five and he died in his fifties. I'm a lucky guy."

(4) Mr. M.M. is fifty years old. He is a lineman with a telephone company.

"In 1963, when I was thirty-eight, I had my first heart attack. I had given blood that afternoon and I guess that had something to do with it. I had never had any chest pain before that attack.

"I was in the hospital for four weeks.When I got out I was fine and I went back to work. Even went back to climbing. Didn't have any pain.

"Then, in 1972, I had a second attack. I was playing bridge with my doctor at the time. He stuck me right in the hospital and I was there for another four weeks. When I got out my doctor sent me to a heart specialist and he decided I should have an angiogram. The angiogram showed that all three of the main blood vessels to my heart were blocked. They advised surgery and in May of 1972, when I was forty-seven, it was done. They took a vein out of my leg and did what they call a triple by-pass."

"How have you been since the operation?" I asked.

"Haven't had a problem. I did give up climbing, but I still

214

work every day. I do a lot of hunting and fishing and I never have any trouble. Doc tells me I'm just as good as normal."

(5) Mr. S.G. is sixty-one. He works as a "parts man" in an auto supply store.

"I had a bad heart attack in 1971," he told me. "I was in the hospital for thirty-nine days and out of work for three months. Even then, when I went back to work I kept having trouble. All I had to do was walk fast or lift something heavy and I'd get a pain in my chest. I was afraid I'd lose my job.

"After another couple of months my doctor finally sent me to a heart specialist. He examined me and thought I ought to have an angiogram. He didn't think a stress test would tell us enough because of my heart attack. The angiogram showed that two of my arteries were blocked, one about ninety-five percent and the other about eighty percent.

"In July of 1972 I had the operation. They took a vein out of my leg and put in two by-passes. I had the operation on a Monday and on Wednesday I had to go to the bathroom real suddenly so I just got out of bed and went. The nurses got all excited but I just hadn't had time to call anyone. It didn't really hurt that much.

"Two months after the operation I was back at work and haven't had a single pain since."

"You're pleased with the results of the operation?" I asked.

"I sure am. I only wish I'd had it before that first attack. Of course, there was no way of knowing I needed it then."

It cheered me to talk to these patients as it did to read of the tennis professional who had a by-pass operation in 1972 and who, three years later, is still teaching and playing tennis eight hours a day. I was also delighted to learn that Judge Stevens, recently appointed to the Supreme Court, had a by-pass done in 1974 and is back playing golf and tennis, swimming, and flying his own Cessna, to say nothing of the stress he continues to put himself under as a tournament bridge player; there are few more competitive arenas than those in which bridge tournaments are played. By comparison, he should find it relaxing to sit on the Supreme Court.

Knowing that others have gone the same route I went, with great success, is very reassuring.

Epilogue

December 17, 1975

(a little more than five months after my heart operation)

I feel fine.

For the first five weeks I was home, the last week of July and all of August, Joan and I lived at our cottage on Lake Minnebelle, six miles out of town. I was weak, as is anyone who has been in a hospital for three weeks but I began exercising immediately. I started by walking just a hundred yards, twice, my first day home, and within a week I was walking a mile three times a day. After three weeks I began to jog. At first I would alternately run and walk in hundred-yard stretches—the so-called Boy Scout's pace—but by my

217

eighth week I was running quarter-mile stretches, and at ten weeks I could run a half mile straight out. I'd do this three times a day. After three months I was running a mile twice a day. I wasn't setting any records for speed, but I wasn't having any discomfort either.

During August I spent most of the day writing and reading. Every afternoon I'd sleep for an hour. In the evening we'd sometimes go out to a movie or to visit friends, but generally I'd get to bed around eleven.

On September, seven weeks after my operation, we moved from the lake back into town and I resumed my surgical practice.

I found that if I did two big cases in one day—for example, a cancer of the bowel and an open reduction of a hip fracture—I'd be quite tired when I was through. The sheer physical exertion might have been part of the reason, but I think emotional stress was a more important factor. I hadn't realized, before my operation, how wearing major surgery can be, on the surgeon as well as on the patient. I was so accustomed to performing surgery that I never noticed the stress. By October 1 I could manage two or three cases with relative ease.

Unfortunately, as soon as I resumed my surgical practice, my blood pressure started to creep up. It had stayed at normal levels on minimal medication during the seven weeks I'd spent recuperating.

I called Roman and told him what was happening. "I expected you'd have that problem, Bill," he said. "High blood pressure is like diabetes. It's very easy to treat in a hospital, but once the patient is out in the world, back to regular living, the problems begin. But don't worry—we've got lots of effective medication we can use." So I added new pills to my regimen and my blood pressure came back under control.

Let me say here that I don't like taking pills. It's annoying to have to remember to take them once or twice or three times a day. But I tried taking a nap twice a day and I tried meditation, to no avail. If I were to quit practicing surgery—if I were to take a job with very little stress—I might be able to keep my blood pressure at normal levels without medicines. But I am a type A personality—a competitive person—and I have no desire to live a sedentary life. If pills can keep my blood pressure normal and still permit me to lead an active life, then I'll take the pills.

Most patients who have heart attacks go through a period of depression following their recovery. Usually the depression lasts about a year; then, if they are feeling good and have gone back to their jobs (or if that has become impossible, at least once again become active members of society at large), the depression dwindles away.

Patients who undergo heart surgery generally follow a similar pattern. Depression, lasting about a year, is a common sequence of the operation. The depression is caused by the knowledge that (1) you have been awfully close to death (technically, if we still defined death as "stoppage of the heart," you actually have been dead), and (2) you are never going to be quite the same again (you will never again be "normal," anatomically speaking, as you were before the operation).

Fortunately, though I've had a few "down" days since my operation, I can't say that I've been really depressed, certainly not to the extent that it has reportedly occurred in most patients who have gone through open-heart procedures. I attribute my lack of depression in part, certainly, to

219

the fact that my postoperative course has, so far at least, been very smooth; actually, I feel as if I am now a much healthier individual, much less likely to die of a heart attack, than was the case before my operation. The doctors who supervise my care agree.

Sometimes I have the feeling that people who know me now look at me and think, "There's Bill Nolen. He's had his heart operated on. He's not quite normal anymore." The feeling that people look on me as "different" bothers me. I know it's silly, and Joan assures me that my friends don't think of me in that way, and I'm grateful for her reassurance. It would upset me if I felt that in any sort of competition, physical or otherwise, my competitor felt an obligation to "take it easy" on me. I'd guess that with time I'll realize that isn't going to happen: that no one is going to give me a break just because I've had a heart operation.

Certainly, now that I think of it, no one gave Lyndon Johnson or Eisenhower a "break" in the political wars just because they'd had heart attacks. And—an idea that buoys me up even more—no woman has apparently found any reason to reject Peter Sellers as a sex partner even though his heart stopped five times a few years back. I'll have to remember that the next time I begin to feel sorry for myself.

Another thing that often happens after recovery from a major illness is that the patient goes back to the life-style that got him into trouble in the first place; the smoker gets over pneumonia and lights up again, the alcoholic's liver disease improves and he starts drinking, and the heart patient, once he feels well, starts eating, drinking, and living just as he did before he had trouble. We have very short memories.

220

I haven't been a complete exception to that rule, but—particularly in the areas which seem to me most important—I haven't done badly.

I have not, for example, gained any weight. Approximately five months after my operation, my weight remains between 170 and 175, about 25 pounds lighter than I was when I first entered the Massachusetts General Hospital.

I've managed this by sticking reasonably close to a schedule. I eat three times a day and don't eat excessively at any meal. Breakfast is usually cold cereal with a banana; lunch is an omelet (made with egg substitute) or a sandwich; dinner is whatever the rest of the family is having.

I used to prefer to eat late—anywhere from seven thirty till nine thirty—and while waiting to eat, I'd nibble on cheese, salami, crackers and whatever else was in the refrigerator. I'd also have three or four drinks.

Now I eat at six or six fifteen, whenever the kids get home from hockey practice, swimming meets or whatever it is they've been doing. Between five fifteen and six fifteen I keep busy, so that I'm not tempted to nibble. And if I have a drink, it's iced tea. I am so used to this schedule that if I don't eat by six thirty I get terribly hungry.

After dinner, while I sit and read, I may have a couple of scotch and waters. Drinking after dinner, for those who want to drink at all—and I do—offers two advantages over predinner drinking. First, I drink less. Second, I don't get that overwhelming tired feeling that I used to get after dinner if I'd had three or four predinner drinks. I get a lot more out of reading in the evening than I used to.

I am not as rigid about what I eat as I was in the first few weeks after my operation. My cholesterol levels are invariably in the low-normal range, so I allow myself to eat eggs occasionally, usually when I'm eating breakfast out. But since the fake eggs work well in omelets, I stick with them when I'm home.

I've found cheeses that are 85 to 95 percent fat-free and that taste pretty good, so we keep them in stock; as well as the 100 percent cholesterol-free mayonnaise that I mentioned earlier. Joan buys tuna fish that's packed in water instead of oil. I've even found peanut butter that has neither salt nor any saturated fats. (You see, even though I know, rationally, that low-cholesterol diets aren't definitely beneficial, I can't shake the emotional bias I have in their favor.) Since I tend to run a slightly elevated triglyceride level, I stay away from sugar. Sugar substitutes are fine on cereal, and I've never been much for desserts anyway.

Actually, none of these dietary changes has bothered me at all. In fact, it has been a revelation to me to find how easy it is to stay on a low-sugar, low-cholesterol diet without making any painful sacrifices. Incidentally, a low-sugar, low-cholesterol diet almost invariably is a low-calorie diet as well.

Let me admit that I have, on occasion, gone off my diet. It's very difficult when eating out to stick to my routine. But an occasional digression doesn't do any harm. Except, on those few occasions when—as in the old days—I drink too much. Then I pay, as does anyone who drinks too much, with a hangover.

On October 8, approximately three months after my operation, I went back to Minneapolis and had another stress test.

I dreaded it. I knew I could run a half mile without any trouble, but I was still concerned that the electrocardiogram would show changes when I was running on the treadmill. I took a sleeping pill the night before the test.

The stress test was completely normal. In June, when I'd first taken it, significant changes had occurred after two minutes of running. This time I ran for seven minutes, got my pulse up to 140 a minute, and there were no changes at all on my EKG. The only reason I quit at 140 was that I was too tired to go on; I had no pain, no shortness of breath, none of the distress I'd had before operation. Both Joan and I were delighted. This time the ride back to Litchfield from Minneapolis was a very happy one.

The day after my stress test I played my first postoperative game of racquetball. I was back on the court where the whole damn nightmare had begun. I was tense at first, worried that I might have trouble, but once I got into the game I relaxed. It was a tough match, but I had no pain and never had to take a break.

To my great delight, despite my four-month layoff, I won.

And I haven't stopped since.